VISIBLE
LEARNING

FOR **SCIENCE**

GRADES K–12

VISIBLE LEARNING

FOR SCIENCE

What Works Best
to Optimize
Student Learning

GRADES K–12

JOHN ALMARODE · DOUGLAS FISHER
NANCY FREY · JOHN HATTIE

CORWIN
A SAGE Publishing Company

FOR INFORMATION:

Corwin

A SAGE Company

2455 Teller Road

Thousand Oaks, California 91320

(800) 233-9936

www.corwin.com

SAGE Publications Ltd.

1 Oliver's Yard

55 City Road

London EC1Y 1SP

United Kingdom

SAGE Publications India Pvt. Ltd.

B 1/I 1 Mohan Cooperative Industrial Area

Mathura Road, New Delhi 110 044

India

SAGE Publications Asia-Pacific Pte. Ltd.

3 Church Street

#10-04 Samsung Hub

Singapore 049483

Program Director: Jessica Allan

Associate Editor: Lucas Schleicher

Editorial Assistant: Mia Rodriguez

Production Editor: Amy Schroller

Copy Editor: Laureen Gleason

Typesetter: C&M Digitals (P) Ltd.

Proofreader: Dennis W. Webb

Indexer: Sheila Bodell

Cover Designer: Rose Storey

Marketing Manager: Maura Sullivan

Printed in the United States of America

ISBN 978-1-5063-9418-3

This book is printed on acid-free paper.

Certified Chain of Custody
Promoting Sustainable Forestry
www.sfiprogram.org
SFI-01268
SFI label applies to text stock

18 19 20 21 22 10 9 8 7 6 5 4 3 2 1

Contents

Visit the companion website at
http://resources.corwin.com/vl-science
to access videos.

List of Videos

Note From the Publisher: The authors have provided video and web content throughout the book that is available to you through QR codes. To read a QR code, you must have a smartphone or tablet with a camera. We recommend that you download a QR code reader app that is made specifically for your phone or tablet brand.

Videos may also be accessed at
http://resources.corwin.com/vl-science

Acknowledgments

We are forever grateful for the teachers and instructional leaders who strive each and every day to make an impact in the lives of learners. Their dedication to teaching and learning is evident in the video clips linked to the QR codes in this book. The teachers at Health Sciences High and Middle College have graciously opened their classrooms and conversations to us, allowing us to make science in the Visible Learning classroom visible to readers. Orange County (Virginia) Public Schools did the same. The students they work with in Orange County Public Schools are better simply because they spent time with the following people:

Cheryl Lamb, Early Childhood Teacher, Gordon-Barbour Elementary School

Alexandra D'Agostino, Fifth-Grade Teacher, Orange Elementary School

Deanna Estes, Earth Science Teacher, Orange County High School

Laura Chambers, Special Education Teacher, Orange County High School

Nick Sodano, Principal, Gordon-Barbour Elementary School

Judy Anderson, Director of Elementary Instruction

Renee Honaker, Director of Secondary Instruction

We are extremely grateful to Dr. Brenda Tanner, Superintendent, for allowing us into the schools and classrooms of Orange County and helping to make our work come alive.

Publisher's Acknowledgments

Corwin gratefully acknowledges the contributions of the following reviewers:

Mandy Frantti, Teacher
Munising Public Schools
Munising, MI

Rita Hagevik, Associate Professor and Graduate Director of
    Science Education
The University of North Carolina at Pembroke
Pembroke, NC

Jane Hunn, Sixth-Grade General Science Teacher
Tippecanoe Valley Middle School
Akron, IN

Debra K. Las, Science Teacher
Rochester Public Schools
Rochester, MN

About the Authors

John Almarode, PhD, has worked with schools, classrooms, and teachers all over the world. John began his career in Augusta County, Virginia, teaching mathematics and science to a wide range of students. In addition to spending his time in PreK–12 schools and classrooms, he is an associate professor in the department of Early, Elementary, and Reading Education and the codirector of James Madison University's Center for STEM Education and Outreach. In 2015, John was named the Sarah Miller Luck Endowed Professor of Education. However, what really sustains John—and what marks his greatest accomplishment—is his family. John lives in Waynsboro, Virginia, with his wife, Danielle, a fellow educator; their two children, Tessa and Jackson; and their Labrador retrievers, Angel and Forest. John can be reached at www.johnalmarode.com.

Douglas Fisher, PhD, is Professor of Educational Leadership at San Diego State University and a teacher leader at Health Sciences High & Middle College. He is the recipient of a William S. Grey Citation of Merit and NCTE's Farmer Award for Excellence in Writing, as well as a Christa McAuliffe Award for Excellence in Teacher Education. Doug can be reached at dfisher@mail.sdsu.edu.

Nancy Frey, PhD, is Professor of Literacy in the Department of Educational Leadership at San Diego State University. She is the recipient of the 2008 Early Career Achievement Award from the National Reading Conference, and she is also a teacher leader at Health Sciences High & Middle College and a credentialed special educator, reading specialist, and administrator in California.

John Hattie, PhD, has been Laureate Professor of Education and Director of the Melbourne Education Research Institute at the University of Melbourne, Australia, since March 2011. He was previously Professor of Education at the University of Auckland, as well as in North Carolina, Western Australia, and New England. His research interests are based on applying measurement models to education problems. He has been president of the International Test Commission, has served as adviser to various ministers, chairs the Australian Institute for Teachers and School Leaders, and in the 2011 Queen's Birthday awards was made "Order of Merit for New Zealand" for his services to education. He is a cricket umpire and coach, enjoys being a dad to his young men, is besotted with his dogs, and moved with his wife as she attained a promotion to Melbourne. Learn more about his research at www.corwin.com/visiblelearning.

Introduction

At 7:55 a.m., Monday through Friday, either my wife or I (John Almarode) drop off our 6-year-old daughter, Tessa, at her elementary school. She is a kindergartener. Our next stop is a local preschool, where we drop off our 3-year-old, Jackson. Science learning is a part of both of their days. As a teacher, I strived to plan, develop, and implement the best learning experiences for each student in my science classroom. As a student, I recall incredibly positive experiences in science throughout my K–12 trajectory. Ms. Cross, my sixth-grade science teacher, inspired me to be a science teacher and then to prepare future science teachers for their own work. As a parent, my hope is that Tessa and Jackson will experience the same rigorous and engaging science learning environment that will encourage lifelong learning in science.

This storyline is a common thread among each of the authors of this book. From John Hattie's son and two daughters-in-law (who are classroom teachers), to Doug and Nancy's mothers (who were both educators), their colleagues, and their students at Health Sciences High and Middle College, we all strive to identify and implement what works best in K–12 science teaching and learning. So, *what does work best in K–12 science teaching and learning?* That is the fundamental question driving the subsequent pages of this book. Answering this question is the goal of this endeavor.

What Works Best Matters

Learners spend approximately 15,000 hours, or 33% of their waking time, in school. Furthermore, schools and teachers are held highly accountable for this time, and thus they strive for at least a year's worth of growth or gains in learning for each of their students. Knowing what works best allows us to be more purposeful and intentional in how we plan, develop, and implement science instruction. John Hattie's research, the research that spawned the concept of *visible learning*, yielded many insights into how we best plan, develop, and implement science instruction. These are three of the most striking insights, or takeaways, from the visible learning research:

1. There are things that we can do in our schools and classrooms that have a negative influence on science learning.

2. There are also things that we can do that have a very small influence on science learning.

3. Finally, there are things that we can do that have a large influence on science learning.

What works best includes the ideas, strategies, interventions, and approaches that have a large influence on student learning in the science classroom. Answering the question of *what works best in K–12 science teaching and learning* requires that we know the differences among these three categories—which is a goal of this book.

In addition to helping administrators and teachers understand the differences in the three previously mentioned categories, John Hattie's 1,400-plus meta-analyses of more than 80,000 studies involving 300 million students revealed one common theme: Science classrooms where *teachers see learning through the eyes of their learners and learners see themselves as their own teachers* provide the greatest learning environments, which are critical to student success in learning science. These classrooms produce visible learners—learners who are (1) active in their learning, so that learning is done *with* them and not *to* them; (2) capable of planning the next steps in their learning and can articulate where they are headed in their learning journey; and (3) aware of what feedback means, can incorporate that feedback into their learning, and know how it informs their learning journey. Building visible learners in the science classroom is also a goal of this book.

What's Coming Next

Over the next several chapters, we are going to focus on aspects of science teaching and learning that are critical for students' success. Each chapter helps answer the question of *what works best*, supports science teachers in their quest to identify *what works best*, and provides a framework for developing visible learners in the science classroom. In each chapter, we will unpack the visible learning research and translate this work into the science learning environment. We will provide clear examples from K–12 science classrooms in which teachers have worked to make learning visible for their students and have impacted learning in significant—and measurable—ways. In other words, these examples, directly observed by the authors, have resulted in student learning. Each chapter includes effect sizes from the visible learning research.

In the first chapter, we provide an overview of the visible learning research and how this research changes the conversation about what happens inside our science classrooms. Specifically, we introduce three phases of learning: surface learning, deep learning, and transfer learning. Given that learning is a process and not an event, this part of the chapter helps us sort through how *what works best* depends on where learners are in the process. Some strategies work best for surface learning, while others work best for deep learning or transfer learning. Learning as a process serves as the organizing concept for *Visible Learning for Science, Grades K–12*. This book focuses on the ways in which teachers can develop students' surface, deep, and transfer learning, specifically by providing students with challenging learning tasks. Teachers have to plan tasks that provide students with opportunities to learn and progress through these stages, as well as the flexibility to return back to different phases of the learning when necessary. The type of task and teacher clarity about these tasks matter as students move along in their thinking from surface to deep to transfer. To design science learning tasks with clarity, teachers have to balance the difficulty and complexity of those tasks. Finally, Chapter 1 opens up the discussion about what visible learning in the science classroom is *not* and the often overlooked role of social skills in the science classroom.

By the end of Chapter 1, you should be able to

1. Explain the key messages from the visible learning research

2. Describe the three phases of the learning process in science

3. Compare and contrast different types of challenging tasks

4. Discuss the role of social skills in science

5. Define and give examples of teacher clarity

Chapter 2 begins the journey through each phase of the learning process. The focus of this chapter is surface learning in the science classroom. Using several examples from K–12 classrooms, this chapter takes an in-depth look at what is meant by surface learning and how to make surface science learning visible. As mentioned earlier, *what works best* depends on where learners are in the learning process. This chapter identifies specific approaches and strategies that foster surface learning of science content and procedural or process skills. We will first guide you in the selection of science learning tasks that promote surface learning, and also discuss surface learning through the processes of science. For example, we focus on direct instruction because of the considerable evidence that direct instruction works. We recognize that there are a lot of science educators who have negative reactions to the phrase *direct instruction*, so we hope you'll allow us to explain why we have included it in a book about science teaching and learning. Direct instruction is not simply telling students what to think or do, thereby robbing them of opportunities to be curious or to inquire about the world around them. When people first hear the phrase *direct instruction,* many of them think of scripted programs that rely on the transmission of information, especially basic skills. Read the section of the text that describes a lesson on energy in organisms and ecosystems and answer the questions at the end of the chapter. Teachers often think of prepackaged curricula that do not take into account the current performance of students or their responses to individual lessons. We don't think of direct instruction in this way. Rather, as John (Hattie) has noted, the essence of direct instruction is actually very common. In his words (2009), "the teacher decides on the learning intentions and success criteria, makes them transparent to students, demonstrates them by modeling, evaluates if they understand what they have been told by checking for understanding, and re-telling them what they have been told by tying it all together with closure" (p. 206). The final section of this chapter will discuss the role of effective feedback at this phase of the learning process.

By the end of Chapter 2, you should be able to

1. Describe what is meant by surface science learning

2. Relate surface learning to science content and process skills

3. Connect teacher clarity to surface science learning

4. Identify learning tasks that promote surface learning in science

5. Explain the role of effective feedback in surface science learning

In Chapters 3 and 4, we turn our attention to deep and transfer learning. Chapter 3 focuses on deep learning, whereas Chapter 4 focuses on transfer learning. In general, the approaches and strategies discussed in these two chapters are more effective for deep and transfer learning than for surface learning. Some of the ideas and examples will likely be familiar to science teachers, while others may be new, as some are drawn from research conducted decades ago. The framework for these two chapters is similar to that for Chapter 2. We will use several examples from K–12 classrooms to take an in-depth look at what is meant by deep and transfer learning and how to make these two phases visible. Again, each chapter identifies specific approaches and strategies that foster deep learning (Chapter 3) and transfer learning (Chapter 4) of science content and procedural or process skills. The final section of each chapter will discuss how effective feedback looks different at each phase of the learning process.

By the end of Chapter 3, you should be able to

1. Describe what is meant by deep science learning

2. Relate deep learning to science content and process skills

3. Connect teacher clarity to deep science learning

4. Identify learning tasks that promote deep learning in science

5. Explain the role of effective feedback in deep science learning

By the end of Chapter 4, you should be able to

1. Describe what is meant by transfer science learning

2. Relate transfer learning to science content and process skills

3. Connect teacher clarity to transfer science learning

4. Compare and contrast the different types of transfer

5. Explain the role of effective feedback in surface science learning

In the final chapter of this book, we focus on how to make science learning visible through evaluation. Visible science learning happens when teachers see science learning through the eyes of their students and students see themselves as their own science teachers. In practice, this requires that teachers are constantly evaluating their impact on student learning, so that they can truly see learning through the eyes of their students. Furthermore, students must have clear knowledge about their own learning, so that they can be active in the learning process, plan their next steps, and understand what is behind the assessment. What does evaluation look like, so that teachers can use this to plan instruction and to determine the impact that they have on learning? As part of this chapter, we continue to highlight the value of evaluation for providing interventions and supports for students that produce growth.

By the end of Chapter 5, you should be able to

1. Calculate an effect size

2. Explain the role of evaluations in visible science learning

3. Describe how evaluating science learning supports all learners as they move through the learning process

4. Summarize the key messages from the visible learning research about what does not work

What Works Best Matters Now

In 2007, Graham Nuthall published a book entitled *The Hidden Lives of Learners*. Analyzing more than 500 hours of classroom video and audio, he stumbled upon some very humbling findings. Two of those findings will help frame the discussion that will unfold in the subsequent chapters:

1. Students already know 60% of what we expect them to learn in our classrooms.

2. A large portion of what happens in our classrooms (80%) is outside the awareness of the classroom teacher.

Nuthall (2007) found that learners come to our schools and classrooms knowing more than we suspect and that there is a hidden world within our classrooms. Now reconsider the amount of time students spend in school (15,000 hours, or 33% of their waking time). This is but a small piece of their time, but it comes with the expectation that they will make significant gains or growth in their learning. Therefore, *knowing and implementing what works best* in science teaching and learning is absolutely essential in maximizing the sliver of time we have with our learners, by ensuring that we focus on what students do not yet know and therefore closing that gap by flipping the 80% to make science learning visible.

Science classrooms where *teachers see learning through the eyes of their learners and learners see themselves as their own teachers* provide the greatest learning environments by incorporating all aspects of science instruction that are critical to student success. These are specific, intentional, and purposeful science learning environments.

All in all, this book contains information on these critical aspects of science teaching and learning that have evidence of their ability to impact student learning at the surface, deep, and transfer phases of the learning process. We're not suggesting that these be implemented in isolation; rather, they should be combined into a series of linked learning experiences and challenging tasks that result in students' engaging in science content and process skills more significantly and better than they had before.

SCIENCE LEARNING
MADE VISIBLE

S pace junk. The Pacific Ocean garbage patch. Climate change. Endangered species. Water. The future of our species is largely in the hands of science, engineering, and technology. The solutions to these crises, and many more, will be solved by scientists who have the cognitive flexibility required to think differently about scientific phenomena and how the world works as a result of these phenomena. To some extent, these three fields have contributed to the very problems that they must now solve. Consider the race to space. Space programs are the crown jewels of industrialized countries, representing a sense of pride and accomplishment. Who would have thought that the *Sputnik* and *Apollo* missions, and the race to communicate worldwide, would eventually result in more than 500,000 pieces of debris orbiting Earth, all traveling at speeds up to 17,500 miles per hour (Garcia, 2016)? These unintended consequences, or side effects, now provide the very questions that current and future scientists and engineers must answer. We could easily explore each of these major issues facing Earth and the millions of species that inhabit the planet, but that's not the point of this book. Rather, the point is that the world needs scientists of all types who demonstrate the cognitive flexibility necessary for tackling the questions, challenges, and crises of the 21st century and beyond. Schools have the responsibility to educate scientists who can collaborate, solve problems, and innovate.

The essential question is this: What is the best way to educate future scientists? And of equal importance: How do we educate members of society so that they understand science, even if they are not going to become scientists themselves? An understanding of science and the processes associated with doing science are not exclusively set aside for those who aspire to be biologists, chemists, geoscientists, or physicists. Scientific literacy, or the knowledge and understanding of the scientific concepts and processes necessary for active engagement in society, is essential for all of us to make informed decisions in our personal lives and when participating in civic, cultural, and economic affairs. Having some understanding of science is part of being an informed citizen. Thus, we really have a dual purpose for this book. We hope to contribute to the conversation about the education of future scientists, especially the types of learning experiences that will prepare them to generate new ideas and solve problems. But we also hope to ensure that the students who graduate from our schools and do not intend to pursue a career in science understand the biological, physical, and social world around them. We want them to be able to think critically about the claims that are made in the media, popular culture, and scientific publications designed for the general public. Take the debate about vitamin C. As Huang and Franzus (1984) note, "the vitamin C debate started at the moment of the discovery of vitamin C" (p. 19). To this day, there are debates about the role of this vitamin in treating a wide range of human conditions, from the common cold to cancer. There is general scientific agreement about the vitamin's role in preventing scurvy, but not in treating other conditions. How does the average person negotiate the conflicting information found on the Internet? How does that person make an informed decision about his or her own personal life? Without a strong grounding in science, neither the future scientist nor the average member of society will be well served by the information from any source.

Much like the vitamin C debate, the world of education has been somewhat adrift and at risk for wide swings across the proverbial pendulum as one study seems to recommend a specific strategy and the next study recommends the exact opposite. For example, in the world of science education, there remains a debate about direct instruction versus inquiry-based approaches. In Dean and Kuhn's words (2007), "Findings revealed that direct instruction seems to be neither a necessary nor sufficient condition for robust acquisition or for maintenance over time" (p. 384). But then Zepeda, Richley, Ronevich, and Nokes-Malach (2015) demonstrated the value of direct instruction in metacognitive skills such as planning, monitoring, and evaluation. As they say, "direct instruction and practice of multiple metacognitive skills can improve metacognitive monitoring, learning, transfer, and motivational outcomes in middle school science class" (p. 966). Who do you believe? What actions do you take to improve students' learning? It seems that there are no clear answers to what works best for students to learn science—which is frustrating, to say the least.

Visible Learning

Enter visible learning. The *Visible Learning* database is composed of more than 1,400 meta-analyses, with more than 80,000 studies and 300 million students (Hattie, 2009, 2012). That's big data when it comes to education. In fact, some have claimed it's the largest educational research database amassed to date. To make sense of so much data, John (Hattie) focused his work on synthesizing meta-analyses. A *meta-analysis* is a statistical tool for combining findings from different studies with the goal of identifying patterns that can inform the collective work of teachers and leaders. In other words, meta-analyses are studies of studies. Consider the use of homework and the influence on student learning. On any given day, administrators and teachers could easily find a study that suggests that homework has a positive influence on student learning. Then the next day, they could find a study that presents an opposite finding. What's a teacher to do? A synthesis of meta-analyses analyzes the collective findings from the studies on homework to unpack the overall trends in these findings. In other words, what does the combined research say, in this case, about homework?

However, the story behind the findings is not solely based on whether findings were positive, were negative, or had no influence on learning. The magnitude of the influence matters as well. The tool that is used to aggregate the information from these combined studies is an effect size. An *effect size (ES)* is the magnitude, or size, of a given effect. Effect size information helps readers understand the impact in more measurable terms. For example, imagine a study in which teaching students science while having them sit on barstools resulted in statistically significant findings ($p < 0.01$, for example). People might remodel all science classrooms to include barstools, and stock in companies that sell these stools to schools would soar. It might even become common and accepted educational practice for all science classrooms to be stocked with barstools.

But then, suppose, upon deeper reading, you learn that the barstools had a 0.03-month gain over the control group, an effect size pretty close to zero. You also learn that the sample size was very large, and the results were statistically significant because of this large sample size, even though the impact was not very valuable. Would you still limit seating in science to barstools? Probably not (and we made up this example, anyway). The takeaway message is that this approach to research helps administrators and teachers make better decisions in their schools and classrooms by focusing on both the impact and the magnitude of that impact.

Understanding the effect size lets us know how powerful a given influence is in changing achievement—or, said another way, the return on investment for a particular approach. Some things are hard to implement in our schools and classrooms and have very little impact. Other things are easy to implement and still have limited impact. To have the biggest impact on student learning in science, we search for things that have a greater impact, some of which will be harder to implement and some of which will be easier to implement. When you're deciding what to implement to impact students' science learning, wouldn't you like to know what the effect size is? Knowing the effect size would allow you to decide whether a particular influence, strategy, or action is worth the effort. But what is the threshold for "worth it" and "not worth it"? John (Hattie) was able to demonstrate that influences, strategies, actions, and so on with an effect size greater than 0.40 allow students to learn at an appropriate rate, meaning at least a year's growth for a year in school. Before this level was established, teachers and researchers did not have a way to determine an acceptable threshold, and thus weak practices, often based on studies that were statistically significant, continued. In other words, teachers and researchers advocated for practices that showed a positive and statistically significant relationship with learning but did not equate to a year of growth for a year in school. Let's take two real examples.

First, let's consider ability grouping. There have been countless numbers of conversations in schools about the best ways to staff classes. To help people understand effect sizes, John (Hattie) created a barometer so that information could be presented visually. The barometer for ability grouping can be found in Figure 1.1. As you can see, the effect size is 0.12, well below the zone of desired effects of 0.40. This is based on 14 meta-analyses, with 500 studies that examined 1,369 effects. Although it's appealing to want to group students by their ability as it is perceived by adults, the evidence suggests that there are more effective ways for impacting students' learning.

Second, let's consider increasing classroom discourse (which is synonymous with classroom discussion or dialogue). Students would be invited to talk with their peers in collaborative groups, working to solve complex and rich tasks. The students would not be grouped by ability, but rather would be grouped by the teacher intentionally to ensure that there is academic diversity in each group as well as language support and varying degrees of interest and motivation. As can be seen in the barometer in Figure 1.2, the effect size of classroom dialogue, or what we prefer to call discourse, is 0.82, well above our threshold, and likely to result in 2 years of learning gains for 1 year of schooling. This finding is generated from 42 studies that examined 42 effect sizes. As a teacher, you would be wise to focus your energy on building classroom discourse rather than focusing on grouping students by ability.

The *Visible Learning* database has been useful in determining what works *best*. A lot of things work. But only some things increase the likelihood

BAROMETER 1: EFFECT SIZE OF ABILITY GROUPING

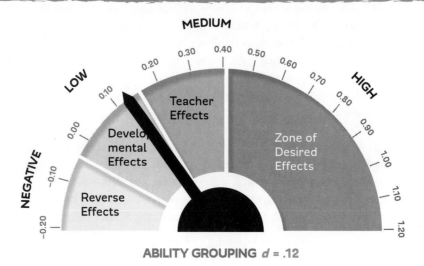

Figure 1.1

that students learn a year's worth of content and thinking skills for a year's worth of schooling. You see, 95% of the things that teachers do work when researchers and educators assume that there will be zero growth. Only a few things work at ensuring that students gain a full year's worth of growth for a year of enrollment in school. And we think it's time that educators focus on what works best, what doesn't work, and what can't hurt. To answer our own questions: What is the best way to educate future scientists, and how do we educate members of society so that they understand science, even if they are not going to become scientists themselves? To accomplish this, we must design learning experiences that implement what works best in the teaching and learning of science. However, this implementation requires that these learning experiences be designed with purpose and intention, driven by where learners start out in their learning and where they need to go next in their learning.

Surface, Deep, and Transfer

The risk of the visible learning list of effect sizes is that administrators and teachers will take a top-10 approach and focus exclusively on those

BAROMETER 2: EFFECT SIZE OF CLASSROOM DISCUSSION

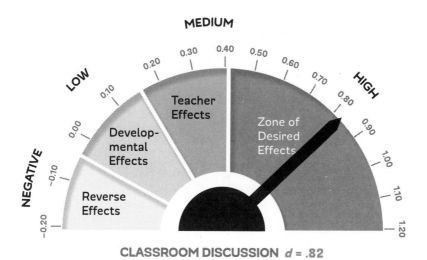

CLASSROOM DISCUSSION *d* = .82

Figure 1.2

influences within that ranking. We don't support this approach because the list does not focus on phases of students' learning. These approaches, strategies, and influences work differentially, based on where students are in their thinking. We think of three levels, or phases, of learning: surface, deep, and transfer (see Figure 1.3). Students must develop surface-level learning if they are ever going to go deep. And with the right instructional moves, deep learning can facilitate transfer.

Learning is a process, not an event. Students understand some science content only at the surface level. As we note in the next chapter, surface learning is often not valued, but it should be and needs to be an essential component of every science classroom. You have to know something about a scientific idea or concept to be able to do something with that idea or concept. We've never met a student who could synthesize information from multiple sources who didn't have an understanding of each of the texts. It's important to note that we do not define surface-level learning as superficial learning. Rather, we define this phase of the learning as the initial development of conceptual understanding, process skills, and vocabulary of a new science topic.

Video 1.1
Visible Learning Defined

http://resources.corwin .com/vl-science

THREE LEVELS OF LEARNING: SURFACE, DEEP, AND TRANSFER

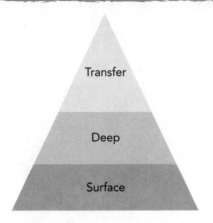

Figure 1.3

With appropriate instruction about how to relate and extend ideas, surface learning becomes deep understanding. Deep understanding is important if students are going to set their own expectations and monitor their own achievement (*ES* = 1.44). Deep learning, which we will discuss in Chapter 3, is when students begin to make connections among conceptual ideas and practice and apply process skills with greater fluency. It's when they plan, investigate, elaborate on their conceptual understandings, and begin to make generalizations based on their experiences with scientific principles and phenomena.

But schooling should not stop there. Learning demands that students be able to apply—or transfer—their content knowledge, process skills, and strategies to new tasks and new situations. The fact that transfer is so difficult to attain is one of our closely kept secrets—so often we pronounce that students can transfer, but too often the processes of teaching them and scaffolding their learning to transfer are not discussed. We will discuss this topic in Chapter 4.

Figure 1.4 contains a representative list of strategies, or influences, organized by phase of learning. We placed each strategy in a specific phase based on the evidence of the strategy's impact and the outcomes that researchers use to document the effect on students' learning. For example, we have included concept maps and graphic organizers under deep learning. Learners will find it hard to organize scientific information or ideas if they do not yet understand that information. For example, without a conceptual understanding of the conservation of energy, high school physics students may classify problems based on surface-level features (i.e., these problems involve a car or a box) instead of deep-level features (i.e., problems where energy and momentum are conserved versus problems where only energy is conserved). When students have sufficient surface learning about specific ideas in science, they are able to see the connections between multiple ideas and create visual representations, which often further illuminate these concepts as scientific principles. There is, however, a group of strategies that have a high impact on student learning, regardless of the particular phase of learning. Providing literacy instruction in science, teachers' expectations, teacher clarity, effective feedback, and student expectations are components of high-impact, high-quality visible learning at the surface, deep, and transfer levels.

Having said that, a key tenant of visible learning is that educators should focus more on learning and less on teaching, and focus specifically and intentionally on the impact that various approaches have on students' learning. Thus, we offer a plea. Please *do not* hold any instructional strategy in higher esteem than students' learning. If a given approach is not working, change it. If you have had success with something in the past, by all means, give it a try, but make sure that it's working. Just because you love visual vocabulary, for example, does not mean that it will work for all students in your science classroom and for all topics in your science curriculum. Teachers have to monitor the impact that learning strategies have on students' science learning and find something that works. Our lists, ideas, and recommendations center around what works best, but they have to work with your students, those sitting in front of you right now. In part, that's why we provide so many options in each phase of learning. There may be no one right way to teach, but there are wrong ways. Our definition of a right way includes evidence that students have progressed in their learning. Students need opportunities to demonstrate their learning so that the learning is visible to both the teacher and the students. Students can do this through a variety of tasks, a topic we will explore next.

Video 1.2
Balancing Surface, Deep, and Transfer Learning

http://resources.corwin .com/vl-science

Challenging Tasks

As we have noted, there are three phases to student learning: surface, deep, and transfer. Teachers have to plan tasks that provide students

HIGH-IMPACT APPROACHES
AT EACH PHASE OF LEARNING

Surface Learning		Deep Learning		Transfer Learning	
Strategy	ES	Strategy	ES	Strategy	ES
Imagery	0.45	Inquiry-based teaching	0.40	Extended writing	0.44
Note taking	0.50	Questioning	0.48	Peer tutoring	0.53
Process skill: recordkeeping	0.52	Self-questioning	0.55	Synthesizing information across texts	0.63
Direct instruction	0.60	Metacognitive strategy instruction	0.60	Problem-solving teaching	0.68
Process skill: organizing	0.60	Concept mapping	0.64	Formal discussions (e.g., debates)	0.82
Vocabulary programs	0.62	Reciprocal teaching	0.74	Organizing conceptual knowledge	0.85
Leveraging prior knowledge	0.65	Class discussion: discourse	0.82	Transforming conceptual knowledge	0.85
Mnemonics	0.76	Organizing and transforming notes	0.85	Identifying similarities and differences	1.32
Process skill: summarization	0.79	Working in small groups in science 0.51			
Integrating prior knowledge	0.93	Cooperative Learning 0.59			
Teacher expectations 0.40					
Feedback 0.70					
Teacher clarity 0.75					
Literacy instruction in science 0.98					
Student expectations of self 1.44					

Figure 1.4

with opportunities to learn and progress through these stages, as well as the flexibility to return to different phases of the learning when necessary. The type of task matters as students move along in their thinking from surface to deep to transfer. To design science learning tasks, teachers have to balance the difficulty and complexity of those tasks. When students experience a "Goldilocks" challenge, the effect size is 0.74—in other words, it is not too hard and not too boring.

To return to the concepts of difficulty and complexity: We think of *difficulty* as the amount of effort or work a student is expected to put forth, whereas *complexity* is the level of thinking, the number of steps, or the abstractness of the task. We don't believe that teachers can radically impact student learning by making them do a lot more work. Similarly, asking students to engage in a task that is far too complex or not complex enough for their current level of thinking can also reduce the impact on student learning. Instead, we should balance difficulty and complexity in the design of learning tasks. Throughout this book, we will return to the concepts of difficulty and complexity as we discuss the various strategies and tasks that teachers use to plan and assess learning. With more and less, or higher and lower levels, of each—difficulty and complexity—four quadrants emerge (see Figure 1.5). Each of these quadrants has an important and necessary role to play in students' learning science content knowledge and process skills.

Video 1.3
Finding the Right
Amount of Rigor

*http://resources.corwin
.com/vl-science*

Fluency

Learners demonstrate fluency in science content and process skills when they automatically utilize this knowledge in future contexts. Fluency is represented by low difficulty and low complexity—this quadrant is not unimportant. Tasks in this quadrant are habits that might still require practice to maintain, but that practice is just for maintenance and not for new learning. For most of the people reading this book, note-taking fits into that quadrant. It's not particularly hard or complex, and it is important. Science teachers likely find demonstrating or modeling the relative positions of the Earth and Sun for each of the four seasons to be relatively easy and to require very little complex thinking on their part. However, this concept is very important to students in the early part of their science learning trajectory. In fact, we believe that the goal is to move everything that we teach in the science classroom into this quadrant. When students develop habits, or fluency, with science concepts and process skills, they are more likely to transfer their learning to new situations. Said differently, if certain content and processes are

COMPARING DIFFICULTY
AND COMPLEXITY

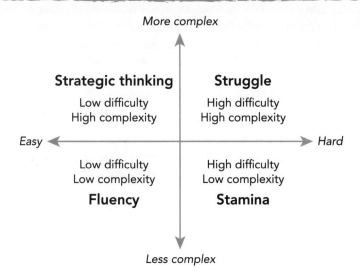

Figure 1.5

automatic, the student can direct more of his or her cognitive energy into the flexibility of this knowledge for new contexts (e.g., direct and indirect Sun rays, climate and weather patterns, and the phases of the Moon). Thus, science classrooms should regularly require students to engage in fluency-building activities that support the development of this automaticity in science.

Here are a few other examples of fluency tasks:

1. Use gestures or dances to help learners remember processes such as the water cycle, the rock cycle, and so on.

2. Ask learners to develop flash cards with a question on one side of the card and the answer on the other side of the card. Learners can do quick checks throughout the day or class period. Note that even though a student may get a question correct, the card should go back in the deck.

3. Spiral science learning throughout the week, semester, and year. Concepts and processes learned two weeks ago should be included in subsequent assessments. Whether you are

using a quick entrance or exit ticket, a traditional test, or a performance-based assessment, the task should pull from previously learned science content knowledge and process skills.

Although fluency is critical, if fluency tasks are all that students experience in science, learning isn't likely to be robust. Instead, learners will resort to rote memorization, which may help them perform on an assessment but will not carry their learning beyond the classroom door on test day.

Stamina

Tasks that are more difficult but not very complex are also important. Tasks of this nature push on students' stamina, grit, and perseverance. For many students, research papers fit into this quadrant. When they are assigned a research paper, students have to plan their approach, identify their central idea, find and cite sources, outline and draft their paper, and revise their text based on feedback from peers, teachers, or themselves. The process for completing a research paper is not that complex, but it can be difficult. As another example, a middle school science teacher asks her students to estimate the number of stars that are visible in the night sky using a cardboard tube. This requires asking her learners to take their cardboard tubes home, wait until the sun sets, and count the number of stars visible through the cardboard tube at eight different locations in the night sky. Plugging a series of numbers into a simple formula provides an estimate of the number of stars. This activity is not very complex, but the counting of stars and the crunching of numbers can be difficult. As with the research paper, students develop the stamina for scientific data collection in field-based sciences.

Here are additional examples of stamina tasks:

1. Engage students in laboratory investigations that ask them to experimentally calculate known constants (e.g., acceleration due to gravity, coefficients of static and kinetic friction, the Hubble Constant, the speed of light, etc.)—yes, known constants. This builds stamina in the scientific process necessary for discovery and innovation.

2. Use performance-based tasks or projects. Ask learners to construct a complex machine—that is, the combination of two or more simple machines that accomplishes a specific task. Or ask learners to develop persuasive essays arguing a particular viewpoint

about climate change, nonrenewable energy, building and living in flood zones, and so forth.

3. Use a weeklong, semester-long, or yearlong investigation to guide science learning. Learners could grow a bean plant, measure the angle of the Sun in the sky, keep a Moon observation journal, develop and maintain a class garden, and so on.

With time, practice, and feedback, tasks that are in the stamina quadrant should move to the fluency quadrant, which is our goal. A key to teaching students to engage in stamina-related tasks is to ensure that the complexity is not so great that students are unable to complete the assignment or task.

Strategic Thinking

Reducing the difficulty and increasing the complexity requires strategic thinking, and often metacognitive thinking as well. When a student rechecks data because the measured current through a resistor does not look right, rereads an article to identify the author's claim because she has questions about the supporting evidence, or slows down in a laboratory investigation to think about each step in the titration process, strategic thinking is being used by the learner. Strategic thinking is especially important for students to develop their scientific inquiry skills. At some point in your life, you did not know how to make inferences from data. Maybe a teacher designed a task for you to try it out. Perhaps a teacher modeled it for you or a peer explained her thinking. Regardless, you were able to experience an inference. Then, rather awkwardly, you began to try out this process. You slowed down, you were consciously aware of what you were trying to do, and you were very deliberate. Over time, and with practice, you internalized the process of making inferences to the point that it became a habit, automatically used. But when things get tough, you return to strategic thinking to solve problems that are elusive. As second graders progress in their ability to ask high-quality science questions, questions that are testable and verifiable through an experiment, their teacher provides several examples and non-examples of high-quality science questions. She asks her students to sort these questions into one of the two categories: examples and non-examples. Working collaboratively, learners begin to think strategically about the characteristics of high-quality questions, self-questioning, self-monitoring, critically thinking, evaluating, and reflecting about what does and does not make a high-quality question in science.

Additional examples of strategic thinking tasks include the following:

1. Provide learners with data and a physical scenario that do not match. Ask learners to critically evaluate both the data and the physical scenario to determine what specifically does not match and why.

2. As students engage in problem solving, reduce the number of problems and have them write out explanations or justifications for each step of the problem-solving process. Another version of this would be to give them problems that are incorrectly solved and ask the leaners to evaluate the decisions made by their peers and correct the errors.

3. Create anchor charts that show a particular comprehension strategy (e.g., summarize, question, connect, predict, visualize, and infer). As learners engage in reading in science, or reading scientific content, model how to utilize the strategies and then expect learners to do the same. Interactive science notebooks work well for supporting strategic thinking.

A key to teaching students to think strategically is to reduce the difficulty, so that the complexity becomes obvious. In the example of high-quality science questions, the teacher would need to reduce the difficulty of questions so that her second graders could focus on the complexity of comparing the essential characteristics of each question.

Struggle

When both difficulty and complexity are high, students are likely to struggle—and struggle is important to the learning process. That's not to say that all lessons and tasks should be a struggle for students, but rather that teachers should strategically place students in situations that require struggle so that they can extend their learning. As Kapur (2008) noted, productive failure is an important consideration in effective learning. Kapur (2014) further observed, "Learning from mistakes, errors, and failure seems intuitive and compelling. Everyone can relate to it. But if failure is a powerful learning mechanism, why do we wait for it to happen? Why can't we design for it, understand how and when it works? What if designing for failure while learning a new concept or skill could result in more robust learning?" (para. 1). For example, learners in a high school physics class are working on an open-ended problem that asks them to consider how the starting height and initial velocity of an object influence the projectile motion of that object. They are provided multiple supplies (e.g., objects of different masses, plastic tracking, measuring devices, etc.), but they are asked to design their own experiments to answer the question. This is both a difficult and a complex task.

When students are engaged in this specific struggle, their physics teacher can and should monitor their conversations and progress toward answering the question so that they can both identify a struggle and then determine what caused the struggle. Only then can the teacher identify appropriate learning experiences to reduce the struggle in future experiences. This monitoring and purposeful intervention allows teachers to move the task to a strategic thinking or stamina task, which requires additional practice and feedback to attain mastery, or fluency. In other words, struggle is important, but students also require opportunities to practice if they are going to ever become proficient in specific content or with a specific process skill. Using struggles to guide subsequent task selection offers learners the opportunity to engage in spaced practice. If the struggle in the previously mentioned physics class is caused by learners not understanding the relationship between horizontal and vertical motion in projectiles, their teacher should provide additional learning experiences to strategically think about this relationship and then practice identifying, describing, and explaining the relationship to increase fluency. And we know that spaced practice is much more effective than mass practice ($ES = 0.71$).

We can create learning situations that promote struggle through the following strategies:

1. *Contrasting cases:* Contrasting cases provides two examples or scenarios related to a scientific idea or phenomenon. The differences between each of the examples are also essential and specific characteristics of the idea. These differences can be very hard to identify for some learners and thus promote struggle (e.g., the concept of change and transformation, metals versus nonmetals, types of muscles, types of chemical reactions, different species, physical adaptations, etc.). Learners will likely struggle to identify the essential characteristics that make the first example different from the second example. When learners do identify these characteristics, add a third example. Contrasting cases help learners notice important but often subtle details.

2. *Deep analogies:* These analogies ask students to find similarities between two or more examples that appear very different on the surface. For example, learners may be asked to find the analogy between speed and density. This forces students to look at the deep structure of concepts and ideas, likely leading to struggle.

Task design is an important consideration in the visible learning science classroom. Students need to experience a wide range of tasks if they are going to become consumers and producers of accurate scientific information. They need opportunities to work with their teacher, with their peers, and independently so that they develop the social and academic skills necessary to continue to learn on their own. This is why science education has to be more than demonstrations, labs, and experiments. After all, bench scientists (i.e., those who conduct research in a laboratory) don't spend their whole day doing experiments. Rather, they spend considerable amounts of time reading, writing, and talking with other scientists.

Science Is More Than Demonstrations and Labs

Perhaps there is no content area more perfectly suited to classroom demonstrations than science. A jaw-dropping demonstration can provoke wonder and inquiry and establish real purpose to subsequent study of a scientific concept. These memorable occasions can also be considered discrepant events because they use the element of surprise to motivate. They may be considered visual displays as well because they activate memory and retention through motion and light. We suspect that inside every good science teacher there is a young child who was mesmerized by a dazzling display of a mysterious scientific concept. In his autobiography, *Uncle Tungsten: Memories of a Chemical Boyhood*, Oliver Sacks (2001) recounts life in a household surrounded by parents and siblings deeply involved in the sciences. In a chapter titled "Stinks and Bangs," he writes of a demonstration that he performed as a 10-year-old with his two older brothers:

> Attracted by the sounds and flashes and smells coming from my lab, David and Marcus, now medical students, sometimes joined me in experiments—the nine- and ten-year differences between us hardly mattered at these times. On one occasion, as I was experimenting with hydrogen and oxygen, there

Video 1.4
Student Engagement Through Active Learning

http://resources.corwin .com/vl-science

was a loud explosion, and an almost invisible sheet of flame,
which blew off Marcus's eyebrows completely. But Marcus
took this in good part, and he and David often suggested other
experiments. (p. 77)

Chemistry teacher Jeff Calihan uses the "stinks and bangs" of science
to motivate and stimulate interest in chemistry. A member of the local
American Chemical Society, he recruits eighth graders from middle
schools to foster their interest in science. He brings a "day of magic" to
each feeder middle school and proceeds to dazzle the students with a
range of demonstrations of chemical wonders, always connecting them
to the scientific concepts that explain the phenomena.

Many of these same students sign up for chemistry when they reach
eleventh grade, enticed by the memory of amazing demonstrations and plenty of stinks and bangs. On the first day of the course,
Mr. Calihan sets a tone for the "Cardinal Chemists," his nickname
for those enrolled in his course. While he introduces the rules of the
class, he pours a small amount of isopropyl alcohol (2-proponol) into
an empty 5-gallon water cooler container. Without explanation, he
lights a match at the mouth of the jug and a loud "boom" results,
followed by the startled gasps and squeals of his new students.
Mr. Calihan then instructs the students to quickly write about what
they have just witnessed. After inviting responses from the students,
he prompts a discussion on the difference between an explosion and
a burn, terminology many of them have just used interchangeably.
Mr. Calihan then gives the students a few minutes to revise their writing by using accurate vocabulary and reviews the rules again, remind-
ing them that they exist for the safety of all. Finally, he moves in for
the final point—"Chemistry is a bomb!"

It is important to note that Mr. Calihan's teaching is not all "stinks and
bangs." He pairs writing with the demonstrations to give students an
opportunity to clarify their understanding and support their inquiry of
what is still unknown to them. He is also careful to ground his work
in the theoretical underpinnings of each demonstration. Indeed, without this careful attention to the scientific concepts, students are likely
to form misconceptions about what they have seen. But the powerful
responses to activities like this one are part of the instructional reper-
toire of this teacher. "Science is fun," says Mr. Calihan, "and there's a
reason why it should grab their attention."

Freedman (2000) recommends several principles for designing effective science demonstrations:

- *Establish a clear purpose.* The demonstration must be directly related to the scientific concepts being studied. This purpose must be made explicit and visible to the learners.

- *Plan the demonstration carefully.* This is more than just assembling the materials. What other learning experiences will the students have in order to understand the theoretical basis for the demonstration? Plan the related lessons to support student connections to important concepts. In fact, make sure you select the demonstration after setting the learning intentions and success criteria, rather than selecting an "awesome" demonstration and making it fit into the content.

- *Plan for repeatability.* Students may need to see the demonstration again. Be sure to have extra materials on hand for this possibility. Also be sure that the demonstration you've selected yields reliable and consistent results. Repeating the demonstration at the end of the lesson can support the consolidation of learning.

- *Plan for safety.* Although discrepant events such as science demonstrations can enhance learning, your students don't need to witness you getting hurt.

- *Consider visibility.* A crowded classroom can make it difficult to see and fully appreciate the demonstration. It can become a safety issue as well for your students if they are jockeying for position. If the sight lines are obstructed in your classroom, consider dividing the class in half and performing the demonstration twice. If the phenomenon you are demonstrating needs to be seen from close range, perform the demonstration with small groups of students.

- *Don't discount the importance of showmanship.* The literal and figurative "stinks and bangs" of science demonstrations can intrigue your students. Don't be afraid to play it up—your enthusiasm is infectious.

Yes, demonstrations are an important aspect of the science classroom that provide a concrete experience that students can relate to more abstract ideas. But students need more than demonstrations to learn content at the surface, deep, or transfer level. The use of demonstrations

Video 1.5
Making Meaning of Science Learning

http://resources.corwin .com/vl-science

without much impact on learning is not isolated to the secondary classroom. Using food to model the parts of a cell, the different types of soil, or the phases of the moon, to name just a few examples, may not produce the desired learning gains if students are not supported with additional opportunities to clarify their understanding and support their inquiry of what is still unknown to them.

We are concerned that, in some circles, science education is seen as a series of experiments and experiences, rather than a purposeful exploration of ideas, skills, and strategies, including social skills. We see the science classroom as an ideal place for students to develop their soft skills, which Google defines as "personal attributes that enable someone to interact effectively and harmoniously with other people." Soft skills typically include

- Teamwork and collaboration
- Adaptability
- Problem solving
- Critical observation
- Conflict resolution
- Situational awareness

A science curriculum devoid of social skills results in knowledgeable individuals who do not know how to get along with their coworkers (i.e., they lack the ability to engage in teamwork and collaboration). Importantly, individuals with low science skills but high social skills gain more and better employment than those who have high science skills but low social skills (Deming, 2017). In other words, many employers are very willing to hire people who have social skills and some science knowledge over individuals who have low social skills but know a lot about science. Imagine what will happen when we create students who have high science content knowledge, strong process skills, and strong social skills! As reported in the *Economist* (Deming, 2017), there is a growing importance of social skills in the workplace (see Figure 1.6); we discuss these skills in more detail in the following section.

The Role of Social Skills in Science

Schools do more than provide academic experiences for students. They also help students develop soft skills. In general, soft skills help someone interact in positive, prosocial, and even harmonious ways with other

THE GROWING IMPORTANCE OF SOCIAL SKILLS

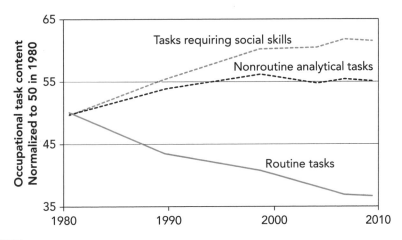

Source: Deming (2017).

Figure 1.6

people. Soft skills are critical during the interview process and often open other doors to new opportunities through future promotions and collaborations. The lack of soft skills puts people at risk for under- and unemployment. There is no official list of soft skills that students must develop, but here are some to consider:

- Communicating, verbally and nonverbally, with others
- Demonstrating commitment and perseverance
- Flexibility and adaptability, especially to stressful situations and changing demands
- Time management and task monitoring
- Leadership, taking responsibility for tasks, and motivating others
- Creativity and problem-solving skills
- Teamwork and collaborative efforts

There are certainly a number of valuable soft skills that we have left out, but you get the point. These skills are not clearly identified in any set of

Video 1.6
Discussion in the Science Classroom

http://resources.corwin .com/vl-science

standards. Rather, they are habits that students need to develop to succeed in life. Schools provide students with the opportunity to practice and learn these soft skills.

The staff at Harbor Middle School are very focused on the development of soft skills for their students. As the principal noted, "When visitors come to our school, they are always impressed by the behaviors they see in our students. Visitors typically comment that these students are ready for adulthood and their careers. We have worked hard in identifying these types of skills that our students need and then building those needs into the flow of the classrooms."

These efforts were evident in visits to the classrooms at Harbor Middle School. In a life science classroom, students were reminded to manage their time so that their tasks were complete. In an earth science classroom, students were working on a complex problem that involved composting and, when asked, they said that they had been working on it for two days and that they believed that they were nearing completion of the project. Another group of students were working collaboratively and provided each other with feedback on their contributions to the group. In every classroom, evidence of the focus on soft skills was obvious.

Efforts to develop soft skills are not limited to adolescents. The staff at Harriet Tubman Elementary School identified specific soft skills that they wanted their students to practice at each grade level. For example, the primary grade teachers focused on turn taking, active listening, and asking topically related questions. The third-grade teachers focused on students' managing their materials, reaching agreements, sharing their opinions with others, and accepting and responding to criticism. This continued across the grade levels, with the school building a number of habits with their students.

For example, in Jason Harp's fifth-grade classroom, students were working on a group project. They were reminded that they were working on their leadership skills, which included

- Seeking feedback from others
- Maintaining a positive work environment
- Following instructions and asking clarifying questions
- Showing initiative

When asked, every student in the room knew what these behaviors were and why they were important. The students talked with a level of sophistication that was impressive. Across the years, their teachers at Tubman Elementary had built their soft skills in such a way that they could interact with others in meaningful ways while remaining focused on the task at hand and maintaining strong relationships. These skills will serve these students well in middle and high school and as they begin their careers, whether or not they enter college.

Each of these previous examples highlights the intentionality of the school and classroom teachers in integrating soft skills into the learning environment. The learning experiences in each of these classrooms purposefully incorporated soft skills into the science learning. These soft skills are valuable because the future scientists in these classrooms need these specific skills to be effective in the various roles they may occupy (university professor, director of a laboratory, science writer, field biologist, science advisor, biomedical engineer, etc.). The work of scientists today demands collaboration and teamwork. For most scientists, the stereotype of a single individual spending his or her entire career isolated in a laboratory, having no contact with the outside world, is simply not accurate. Soft skills are also important because they help students who do not choose to pursue a career in science to work more effectively with others, even on tasks that are not science related. We see science learning as an opportunity to develop and extend students' social skills. In fact, we believe that the social nature of learning is an essential part of what science teachers should teach, which brings us to the topic of teacher clarity.

Teacher Clarity

Teacher clarity is about learning expectations, including the ways in which students can demonstrate their understanding. The effect size is 0.75. Every lesson, regardless of whether it focuses on surface, deep, or transfer learning, needs to have a clearly articulated learning intention and associated success criteria. We believe that students should be able to answer, and ask, these questions about each lesson:

1. What am I learning today?

2. Why am I learning this?

3. How will I know that I learned it?

Video 1.7
Making Learning Clear
for Students

http://resources.corwin
.com/vl-science

The first question requires deep understanding of the learning intention. The second question begs for relevance, and the third question focuses on the success criteria. Neglecting any of these questions compromises students' learning. In fact, we argue that these questions compose part of the Learner's Bill of Rights. Given that teachers (and the public at large) judge students based on their performance, it seems only fair that students should know what they are expected to learn, why they are learning it, and how their success will be determined. The marks teachers make on report cards and transcripts become part of the permanent record that follows students around. Those documents have the power to change parents' perceptions of their child, determine future placements in school, and open college doors. And clarity works. Clearly articulating the goals for learning has an effect size of 0.50. Providing success criteria has an effect size of 1.13. It's the right thing to do, and it's effective.

We're not saying that it's easy to identify learning intentions and success criteria. Smith (2007) notes, "Writing learning intentions and success criteria is not easy . . . because it forces us to 'really, really think' about what we want the pupils to learn rather than simply accepting statements handed on by others" (p. 14). We are saying that it's worth the effort.

Learning intentions are more than a standard. There have been far too many misguided efforts that have mandated teachers to post the standard on the wall. Learning intentions are based on the standard, but they are chunked into learning bites. In too many cases, the standards are not understandable to students. Learning intentions, if they are to be effective, have to be understood and accepted by students. Simply writing a target on the dry erase board and then reading it aloud waters down the power of a learning intention, which should focus the entire lesson and serve as an organizing feature of the learning that students do. At minimum, learning intentions should bookend lessons with clear communication about the learning target early in the lesson and later reference to it as the lesson closes. In addition, teachers can remind students of the learning intention at each transition point throughout the lesson. In this way, the learning intention drives the lesson, and students will develop a better understanding of how close they are to mastering the expectations. Most critically, the learning intention should demonstrably lead to the criteria of success—and if you had to use only one of these approaches, we would recommend focusing on being more explicit about the success criteria; again, the effect size is 1.13. Both help, but the judgment about the standard of work desired is more important

SAMPLE LEARNING INTENTIONS

Grade	Poor Example	Improved Version
K	Compare a push with a pull.	Today, we will conduct an investigation of heavy objects. We'll learn the difference between pushing on these objects and pulling on these objects. What happens when I use a bigger push or a bigger pull?
5	Complete a handout on plant growth.	Today, we will learn how plants acquire the energy they need to grow. How do the great sequoia trees get so big?
7	Determine whether a chemical reaction occurred.	We will understand that chemical reactions result in new substances that have different properties from those of their reactants. We will learn how to know whether a chemical reaction has occurred.
11	Compare different types of electromagnetic radiation.	We will understand that the different types of electromagnetic radiation have distinct characteristics that influence how each type of radiation interacts with other matter and energy.

Figure 1.7

than explication about the particular tasks we ask students to do. It is the height of the bar, not the bar itself, that matters.

Figure 1.7 contains some poorly written learning intentions and some improvements that teachers made collaboratively as they explored the value of this approach. Note that the intentions became longer, more specific, and more interesting. The improved versions invite students into learning. Of course, learning intentions can be grouped. Sometimes an activity can contribute to several learning intentions, and other times a learning intention requires several activities. However, when learning intentions are spread over many days, student interest will wane and motivation will decrease. When teachers plan a unit of study and clearly identify the learning intentions required for mastery of the content, most times they can identify daily targets. In doing so, they can also identify the success criteria, which will allow for checking for understanding and targeted feedback.

The success criteria must be directly linked with learning intentions to have any impact. The success criteria describe how students will be expected to demonstrate their learning, based on the learning intention. That's not to say that success criteria are simply a culminating activity, but they can be. Consider the following ways in which students might demonstrate success based on this middle-grade learning intention: *I understand that the particular phase of matter is related to energy and the movement of the molecules.*

- I can describe the three states of matter in terms of the molecular movement.
- I can explain the relationship between temperature, pressure, and changes in the state of matter.
- I can construct a sequence of models that show the movement of molecules across the three states of matter.
- I can make predictions about a substance's state of matter using information data on pressure and temperature.

This learning intention and the subsequent criteria for success work for multiple learning experiences in this particular classroom. Each statement is more than a task. Therefore, teachers and learners have multiple options for meeting these expectations. Clarity is important!

How learning intentions and success criteria are presented in the classroom is not as important as the necessity for everyone in the classroom to be able to explain what is it that students should be learning, and how they will know whether they learned it (not to mention how the teacher will know this). Figure 1.8 presents several examples of learning intentions and success criteria.

The first example in Figure 1.8 follows the format previously presented in this chapter for success criteria, an "I can" statement. However, there are other ways to make both the learning intention and the associated success criteria visible to learners. The second image uses the phrasing "Today I am . . ." (learning intention) paired with "So that I can . . ." (success criteria). For younger learners, the learning intention can be verbally shared with learners during morning meeting or circle time, and then the success criteria can be visible at each individual learning

a.

> Tues. 4/19 B-day
>
> I can create Transverse and Longitudinal waves with a slinky. I can sketch a transverse wave, and identify and label its characteristics. I can use a Slinky with a partner to create and observe the Doppler Effect.

Image courtesy of Orange County Public Schools

b.

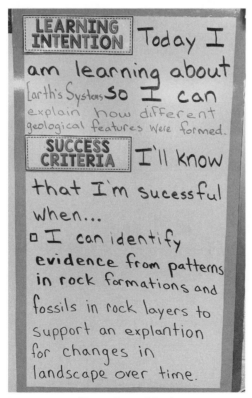

> **LEARNING INTENTION** Today I am learning about Earth's Systems so I can explain how different geological features were formed.
>
> **SUCCESS CRITERIA** I'll know that I'm sucessful when...
> □ I can identify evidence from patterns in rock formations and fossils in rock layers to support an explantion for changes in landscape over time.

Image courtesy of Barren County Schools

(Continued)

c.

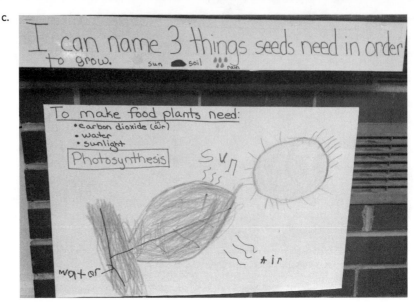

I can name 3 things seeds need in order to grow. sun soil rain

To make food plants need:
• carbon dioxide (air)
• water
• sunlight
Photosynthesis

SUN

water

air

Image courtesy of Orange County Public Schools

d.

Today we will answer...
What are the states of matter?

Image courtesy of Spotsylvania County Public Schools

e.

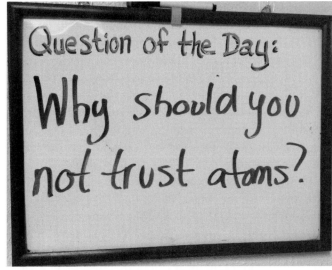

Image courtesy of Spotsylvania County Public Schools

Figure 1.8

center or station. Finally, the last two examples in Figure 1.8 present the learning intention in the form of a question. Successful learning would happen when the student can answer the question of the day. The power of learning intentions and success criteria lies not in the way they are presented or phrased, but in the ability of both the teacher and the learner to know the answers to these questions: What am I learning today? Why am I learning this? How will I know that I learned it?

Importantly, students can be involved in establishing the success criteria, and in many cases the learning intentions. Teachers can ask their students, "How will you know you have learned this? What evidence could we accept that shows that learning has occurred?" In these situations, students can share their thinking about the success criteria, and often they are more demanding of themselves than their teachers are. In a fourth-grade class focused on processes that shape the Earth (NGSS Lead States, 2013), Mrs. Coyner shared with her students that they would be learning how to provide evidence of the effects of weathering or erosion by water, ice, wind, or vegetation. Specifically, her learning intention was this: "I understand that evidence of erosion is an observable process." During this particular class meeting, Mrs. Coyner asked her students to identify several ways in which they would know whether they met this learning intention. Almost immediately, several of her students suggested that they would have pictures to put in their inter-active science notebooks. These pictures could come from the Internet or from their own schoolyard. Others added that they should write an explanation about how each picture would show evidence of erosion. One student suggested that they should review the different factors con-tributing to erosion and talk about possible examples. Specifically, this learner could not remember "about vegetation." Another added that the students should work together in groups so that they could talk about their pictures and "come up with other ideas." This same stu-dent mentioned that they should have assigned jobs within their small groups so that they would not run out of time "like last week." None of these answers were wrong; they all used the learning intention and the co-construction of success criteria to improve the students' collaborative learning time. In this case, the students established the success crite-ria and opened the door to feedback from their peers and their teacher in their successive approximations in demonstrating mastery of their learning.

Further, when students understand the success criteria, they then can be most involved in assessing their own success, and their progression toward this success. A simple tool allows students to put sticky notes in one of four quadrants to communicate their status (see). This alerts the teacher, and other students, about help that is needed. It mobilizes peer tutoring ($ES = 0.54$) and cooperative instead of competitive learning ($ES = 0.54$), and also builds student-centered teaching ($ES = 0.54$).

Clearly articulating the success criteria allows errors to become more obvious. Errors should be expected and celebrated, because they are opportunities for learning. If students are not making errors, they have likely previously mastered the learning intention. Also note that feed-back thrives on the presence of errors. Errors should be the hallmark of learning—if we are not making enough errors, we are not stretch-ing ourselves; if we make too many, we need more help to start in a different place. Unfortunately, in too many classrooms, students who already know the content are privileged, and students who make errors feel shame. In those situations, learning isn't occurring for students who already know the content; they've already learned it. But learning isn't occurring for the students who make errors, because they hide their errors and avoid feedback. Classrooms have to be safe places for errors to be recognized. Coupling clear learning intentions and success criteria

SAMPLE SELF-ASSESSMENT OF LEARNING

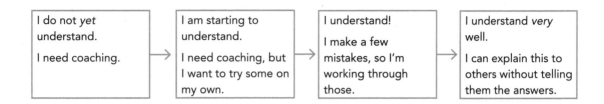

I do not *yet* understand.	I am starting to understand.	I understand!	I understand *very* well.
I need coaching.	I need coaching, but I want to try some on my own.	I make a few mistakes, so I'm working through those.	I can explain this to others without telling them the answers.

Figure 1.9

with a classroom culture that views mistakes as learning opportunities eliminates these scenarios.

For example, a secondary science class was focused on reviewing the changes in climate—there were clipboards everywhere, with students running around the school checking temperatures. They had great analyses and stunning box and whisker plots. But when they were asked how long they had been doing this task, they said three weeks (and that it was fun). What a waste of more than two weeks. In other words, the teacher in this scenario was not receiving the feedback from her learners that they were ready to move on to a more challenging or a new task. Perfection is not necessarily the aim of lessons; the presence of errors is a better indicator of a successful lesson, and this surely hints to the teacher and students the most likely place to go next.

When errors are celebrated and expected, feedback takes hold. Feedback has a powerful impact on student learning, with an effect size of 0.79, placing it in the top 10 influences on achievement. But it's only when the feedback is received that it works. Giving feedback is different from receiving feedback. Feedback is designed to close the gap between students' current level of understanding or performance and the expected level of performance, which we call the success criteria. For feedback to work, teachers have to understand

- Students' current level of performance
- Students' expected level of performance
- Actions teachers can take to close the gap

39

FEEDBACK STRATEGIES

Feedback Strategies Can Vary in Terms of . . .	In These Ways . . .	Recommendations for Good Feedback
Timing	• When given • How often	• Provide immediate feedback for knowledge of facts (right/wrong). • Delay feedback slightly for more comprehensive reviews of student thinking and processing. • Never delay feedback beyond when it would make a difference to students. • Provide feedback as often as is practical, for all major assignments.
Amount	• How many points made • How much about each point	• Prioritize—pick the most important points. • Choose points that relate to major learning goals. • Consider each student's developmental level.
Mode	• Oral • Written • Visual/ demonstration	• Select the best mode for the message. Would it suffice to make a comment when passing the student's desk? Is a conference needed? • Interactive feedback (talking with the student) is best when possible. • Give written feedback on written work or on assignment cover sheets. • Use demonstration if "how to do something" is an issue or if the student needs an example.
Audience	• Individual • Group/class	• Individual feedback says, "The teacher values my learning." • Group/class feedback works if most of the class missed the same concept on an assignment, which presents an opportunity for reteaching.

Figure 1.10

Feedback, as Brookhart (2008) describes it, needs to be "just-in-time, just-for-me information delivered when and where it can do the most good" (p. 1). includes information about the ways in which feedback can vary in terms of timing, amount, mode, and audience. We'll focus on feedback in greater depth in the chapter on deep literacy learning. For now, we hope you appreciate the value of feedback for impacting student learning.

Conclusion

One of the most influential contributions to 20th-century educational theory was the development of the field of cognitive science. Before the advent of cognitive studies, the prevailing learning theory was behaviorism, which concentrated on the role of an outside stimulus as a mechanism for learning. The publication of *A Study of Thinking* in 1956 (revised in 1986; Bruner, Goodnow, & Austin, 1986) led the way for exploration of what happens inside the minds of learners and how they organize and use information. Over the course of the next 60 years, scientists, psychologists, and educators have examined memory, emotion, schema, and experience as essential components of learning. In fact, the influence of cognitive science is so profound that it now may be difficult to conceptualize how the process of learning was perceived in the first half of the 20th century. This book, for instance, is replete with learning approaches that reflect our profession's roots in cognitive science—scaffolding, metacognition, accessing background knowledge, and transferring of learning, to name a few.

Today, we know much more about how students learn. We have at our disposal millions and millions of studies that can guide the work teachers do with students. Visible learning provides a way to understand and mobilize the research, while focusing on what works best. As we explore visible learning for science, we will add an additional aspect. This book is about what works best and when. As we have noted earlier, some instructional strategies are better for surface learning, whereas others are better for deep or transfer learning. Said another way, surface learning strategies don't work any better at developing deep learning than deep learning strategies work to develop surface learning. Our focus is really about what works best and when. To ensure that students develop sufficient knowledge and skills, science teachers have to also develop students' soft skills and ensure that students know what they are supposed to be learning, why they are learning it, and how they will know they've learned it. Visible learning in science is about aligning instruction with the phases of learning, focusing on soft skills, tapping into the power of teacher clarity, and determining the impact on learning (making changes when learning does not occur). Together, these efforts can change the world, because the next generation of scientists will solve the problems we have created today, and the larger population will be more informed about the world around them.

Reflection Questions

1. How would you explain the three phases of learning to a colleague? What role does each play in your science classroom? What has this made you think about in your teaching?

2. What works best in the teaching and learning of science? How do you know?

3. Consider the types of tasks in which you ask your students to engage. Are they aimed at building fluency, stamina, or strategic thinking? In which quadrant are a majority of your tasks found? What changes could you make to a specific fluency task to incorporate more strategic thinking?

4. What would your students say if they were asked, "What are you learning, why are you learning it, and how will you know you have learned it?" How can you ensure that there is more teacher clarity in your science classroom? What role do learning intentions and success criteria play in your classroom?

SCIENCE SURFACE LEARNING MADE VISIBLE

2

Surface learning is an essential and necessary component of the learning process. For learners to effectively engage in deeper learning and then transfer this learning to new and different contexts, they must have acquired and consolidated initial learning of the specific science content and process skills associated with a particular topic. For example, learners must have a conceptual understanding of habitats and relevant process skills (e.g., observing, predicting, inferring, analyzing) associated with habitats in order to engage in deep learning or transfer. This acquisition and consolidation of initial learning should combine learning exploration and teacher-activated instruction (e.g., direct instruction) with an explicit introduction to the structure of the content (i.e., terminology, labels, processes, and procedures). Let's consider the classroom of Angela Cross.

Angela Cross is planning a unit on matter and energy in organisms and ecosystems. Prior to the seventh grade, her learners have had only an introduction to the interdependency between animals and their environments. In third grade, students learned about how animals adapt to changes in the environment (e.g., land characteristics, water distribution, and temperature). The big idea from this prior learning was that some animals survive well, some survive less well, and others do not survive at all (NGSS Lead States, 2013). For the learners in Ms. Cross's classroom, this will be the students' first formal experience with resource availability for organisms and populations of organisms in an ecosystem. As Ms. Cross plans for this unit, she considers her students' progression through the learning process from surface, to deep, to transfer. During this unit, to develop a conceptual understanding of the flow of matter and energy in an ecosystem, her students will first analyze and interpret data on resource availability, model the energy flow among living and nonliving parts of an ecosystem, and construct an argument stating that changes in components of an ecosystem affect populations.

Ms. Cross's learners will build background and vocabulary knowledge so that they can make connections between matter, energy, organisms, and ecosystems. The textbook and associated resources provide a starting point for the learning progression, but Ms. Cross must be very clear about what her students are learning, how best to learn it, and how they will know they have learned it. She must establish clear learning intentions that communicate to the students what they are learning each day. She must also develop clear success criteria that articulate what evidence students must generate to make their learning visible to both Ms. Cross and her learners. Ms. Cross plans her lessons to ensure that by the end of this unit, her learners will be confident that they understand the content, can apply the concepts, and are ready to connect these concepts to future topics.

On Monday morning, students arrive at Ms. Cross's room to find a laminated picture of a panther at each of their tables. Ms. Cross introduces the day's learning by telling her students that they are all going to be panthers; their seats at the tables are their panther dens, and, as predators, they must hunt for their food (adapted from "Panther Hunt," https://www.populationeducation.org). Spread out around the room are small paper cups, turned upside down, with a letter written on the bottom (see Figure 2.1). *S* stands for squirrel, *R* for rabbit, *P* for porcupine, *B* for beaver, and *D* for deer. Of course, there are more of some animals than others. For example, there are only two cups with the letter *D*, but 80 cups with the letter *S*.

Ms. Cross tells her students that this is the habitat of a population of panthers and that each of them represents one panther: "When I say go, each of you will try to find enough food to survive for one month, 50 kilograms." She then directs her learners' attention to the table on the whiteboard (see Figure 2.2).

Ms. Cross continues: "Each panther can carry only one prey at a time, and panthers don't run down prey—they stalk it." Once Ms. Cross says, "Go," the "panthers" stalk around the room, gathering one prey at a time until all the cups are gone. Once all the cups, or prey, have been taken, Ms. Cross asks her learners to find the total kilograms (kg) of food they have collected. The student, or panther, who has collected the cups shown in Figure 2.3 has a total of 32.5 kg.

As a group, learners record their names and data on a class chart, so that the total amount of food collected by each classmate, or panther, and whether each student met the 50-kg requirement for survival is visible to everyone (see Figure 2.4).

At this point in the lesson, Ms. Cross shares the day's learning intention with her students: "Today, we will understand the effects of resource availability on organisms and populations of organisms in an ecosystem." Through this learning intention, Ms. Cross makes it clear what she wants her students to learn or understand by the end of this

PAPER CUPS FROM PANTHER HUNT ACTIVITY

a.

b.

Figure 2.1

particular lesson. She asks her students to discuss how the panther hunt has helped them understand the effects of resource availability. As learners engage in this discussion, Ms. Cross listens in on the conversations, encouraging students to edit or add to their vocabulary graphic organizers. She then shares her criteria for success with the learners: "I will know I have been successful when (1) I can describe how populations of organisms depend on interactions with other living things and (2) I can explain that competition for resources, such as food, constrains population growth."

To focus her students on the intended learning outcomes of this task, Ms. Cross distributes discussion questions and provides time for the students to talk through responses with their neighbors:

PREY CHART FROM PANTHER HUNT ACTIVITY

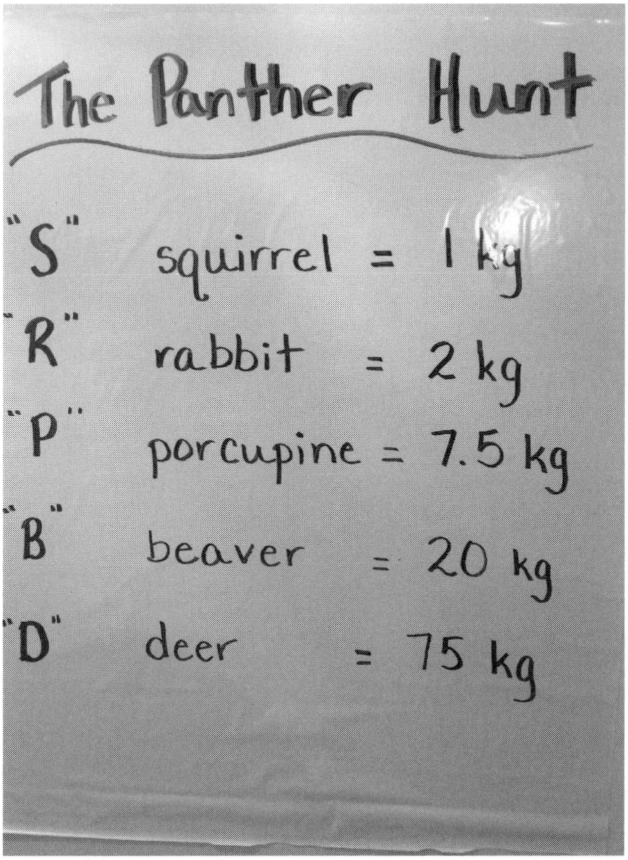

The Panther Hunt
"S" squirrel = 1 kg
"R" rabbit = 2 kg
"P" porcupine = 7.5 kg
"B" beaver = 20 kg
"D" deer = 75 kg

Figure 2.2

1. If more panthers were in our habitat, would this habitat support them? Support your answer. How many kilograms of prey would be needed to support all of the panthers in this habitat?
2. What would happen to the panther population if all the rabbits died of disease? What would happen to the prey animals if all the panthers were captured and removed from the habitat?

Figure 2.3

3. What would happen to this habitat if the water became polluted? Which group of animals would be most affected by the pollution?

4. What other observations did you make while "hunting"? What about the specific location of the "surviving" panthers in the habitat? What is the relationship between your location and your ability to find food?

BLANK CLASS CHART
FROM PANTHER HUNT ACTIVITY

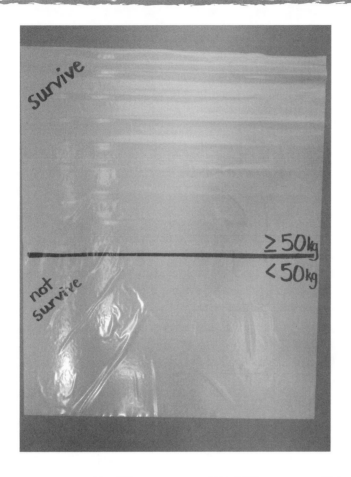

Figure 2.4

Through the class discussion, Ms. Cross facilitates the students' acquisition of key vocabulary associated with this content as they respond to each question. She asks students to summarize the meanings of *habitat*, *predator*, and *prey*, first with their neighbors and then in writing by adding these terms to their vocabulary graphic organizers in their interactive notebooks.

Term	What It Means in My Own Words	Example or Drawing

As students contribute to the discussion, Ms. Cross introduces the concept of resource availability and the flow of matter and energy through an ecosystem. Again, each new term or concept is added to the students' vocabulary graphic organizers, linking the term or concept to a specific example from the panther hunt.

Term	What It Means in My Own Words	Example or Drawing
Predator		
Prey		
Habitat		
Resource availability		
Matter flow and energy flow		

As the lesson comes to a close, Ms. Cross gives each student an exit ticket.

EXIT TICKET

Name: _____   Date: _____

1. Red foxes live mostly in forested areas and build their dens within a few hundred yards of water. They hunt at night, at dusk, or in the early morning hours for rabbits, squirrels, mice, and birds. However, they have a particularly strong appetite for mice. Using this information, respond to the following questions:

   a. How might an increase in the bird population affect the population of red foxes?

   b. Give two additional scenarios that would increase the competition of red foxes for resources.

   c. Explain how these scenarios would increase the competition of red foxes for resources.

This lesson is the result of deliberate, purposeful, and intentional planning by Ms. Cross, where she focuses on the nature of the learning in her students. The lesson is an example of developing surface learning for initial acquisition of conceptual understanding, specifically related to resource availability and the flow of matter and energy in an ecosystem. As students progress in their learning through this unit, they will focus on analyzing and interpreting data on resource availability, modeling energy flow among living and nonliving parts of an ecosystem, and constructing an argument that changes in components of an ecosystem affect populations (NGSS Lead States, 2013). Ms. Cross's decision to engage her learners in the panther hunt task relies on what part of the unit content and which process skills will be an initiation to new ideas requiring students to first develop conceptual understanding and then, at the right time, to be introduced to the labels and procedures that give structure to concepts. This information about Ms. Cross's learners comes from providing the learners with opportunities to make their prior knowledge visible to both their teacher and the other students. When learners are aware of their own prior knowledge, they can better engage in this part of the learning process. What do the students already know about this particular habitat and the organisms or animals found in the panther hunt?

Ms. Cross concludes this particular learning experience by asking her students to consolidate their learning and engage in transfer to a situation that is similar to but different from the one they focused on in class (i.e., panthers to foxes). One strategy for consolidating learning at the surface learning phase entails rehearsal ($ES = 0.73$). Rather than relying on the clock or the bell to indicate the conclusion of class, Ms. Cross actively engages her learners in the consolidation phase of learning through rehearsal of their learning on an exit ticket. This lesson develops conceptual understanding of the language necessary to analyze, interpret, model, and construct arguments. In other words, this is surface learning that students need in their toolbox to build deep understanding and then apply their thinking to new contexts or situations with organisms and ecosystems. Surface learning happens best when teachers employ specific, high-impact approaches that foster initial acquisition of conceptual understanding.

Surface Learning in Science

In the Introduction and Chapter 1, we discussed the boom in scientific knowledge and innovation over the past 15 years. With the ever-increasing complexity in the scientific world, providing a strong foundation through a conceptual understanding of scientific processes, crosscutting concepts, and disciplinary core ideas is essential to supporting learners' progression toward increasing levels of sophistication and application to innovative contexts and problems. At the same time, this foundation should also provide all learners with the conceptual understanding that promotes scientific literacy, which is necessary to engage in important scientific issues as a citizen. To successfully navigate the progression from surface to deep learning, and then on to transfer learning, the timing of specific instructional approaches and strategies is critical. Timing is everything, and the wrong approach or strategy at the wrong time undermines efforts and prevents students from mastering key concepts, strategies, and processes.

Knowing when and how to help a student move from (sufficient levels of) surface to deep learning is one of the marks of expert teachers. Consider the two categories of instructional approaches: *Teaching for Surface Learning* and *Teaching for Deeper Learning* when the initial focus is on learning the content (see Table 2.1).

The *teaching for surface learning* column is associated with higher effect sizes than the *teaching for deeper learning* column. However, inquiry-based teaching and problem-based learning are two instructional approaches commonly associated with effective science instruction. How could this be? The answer is timing. For example, a problem-based learning task that requires students to notice relationships, extend ideas, and make connections to other contexts will not be successful if learners do not have a conceptual understanding of the concepts that they are to relate, extend, and connect. Without the right tools in the toolbox, learners cannot build deep understanding. Placed within the deep learning or transfer phase, the approaches in the *teaching for deeper learning* column will result in greater gains (Hattie & Donoghue, 2016). The effects of many of these methods are larger when introduced after students have sufficient surface knowledge—for example, the effect for problem-based learning moves from .15 to .54 when introduced at the right time. As mentioned in the opening of this chapter, acquisition and consolidation of initial learning should combine learning explora-tion and teacher-directed instruction with explicit introduction to the structure of the content.

Michael Barton wants his students to understand that the six types of simple machines make work easier. Mr. Barton and his students will know they have been successful when (1) learners can describe how each simple machine is used in a specific context and (2) learners can explain when to use specific simple machines (NGSS Lead States, 2013). For Mr. Barton's learners to successfully describe and explain the use of simple machines, they must first have the right tools in their toolbox, specifically, a conceptual understanding of each simple machine and the foundational information about how each one works. Mr. Barton makes a purposeful and intentional decision to teach the targeted knowledge and skills associated with simple machines through direct instruction, worked examples, and mastery learning (i.e., *teaching for surface learning*). He surveys his learners' prior knowledge, shares the success criteria for the day, and then provides a graphic organizer to accompany the lesson.

Mr. Barton proceeds to provide specific examples of each type of sim-ple machine, first asking his students to describe what they see, predict how they might use this simple machine, and then identify a real-world example. The graphic organizer provides a structure for organizing the information. As students receive feedback during this guided practice, Mr. Barton increases both the difficulty and complexity of the learning by providing two examples. Learners are asked to compare and contrast

Teaching for Surface Learning	Teaching for Deeper Learning
Worked examples, $ES = 0.37$	Student control over learning, $ES = 0.02$
Behavioral organizers, $ES = 0.42$	Web-based learning, $ES = 0.18$
Providing goals, $ES = 0.50$	Problem-based learning, $ES = 0.26$
Mastery learning, $ES = 0.57$	Inquiry-based teaching, $ES = 0.40$
Direct instruction, $ES = 0.60$	Inductive teaching, $ES = 0.44$

Table 2.1

Video 2.1
Learning Progressions That Support Teaching and Learning

http://resources.corwin .com/vl-science

the examples based on how the simple machine could be used and in what specific contexts the simple machine would be helpful.

To consolidate their learning, students are placed into cooperative learning groups, and they rotate through a series of learning stations where they are tasked with moving specific objects through a maze or obstacles. They must determine which simple machine most easily accomplishes each task. All the while, Mr. Barton is moving around the room, observing this independent practice, assessing student performance, and providing feedback. The closure for this lesson involves the students' taking time to summarize the targeted knowledge and skills acquired from this learning experience. This is done using the graphic organizer provided at the start of the lesson.

Mr. Barton, using information gained from pre-assessing his learners, recognizes that this is initial learning about simple machines. He has combined learning exploration and teacher-activated instruction with an explicit introduction to the structure of the simple machines and how they make work easier. He has decided not to utilize approaches and practices associated with deep learning because that is not where his learners are in the learning process. Instructional practices that foster deep learning are not the most effective ones to employ when students are still at the surface level of developing understanding of any given science topic.

Consider Ms. Cross's decision to engage her students in the panther hunting task. She could have easily printed off a packet of worksheets that would require the students to complete a series of non-contextual, fill-in-the blank questions or rote memorization of the terms *predator*, *prey*, *habitat*, and *resources*. These are exercises, and fairly meaningless ones. The phrase *surface learning* may hold a negative connotation for many people. It's easy to assume that by "surface," we mean "super-ficial" or "shallow," or that by surface-level learning, we mean rote memorization of procedures and vocabulary that have typically been taught at the beginning of a lesson and are disconnected from conceptual understanding. This is not what we mean by surface learning. Rather, the phrase *surface learning* represents an essential part of learning made up of both conceptual exploration and learning vocabulary and procedural skills that give structure to ideas. Ms. Cross has made an intentional and purposeful decision to engage her learners in a task that provides a context for these terms, concepts, and ideas. This context also encourages students to use a variety of scientific processes and thinking to complete the task. For successful surface learning, the task needs to be one that promotes elaborate encoding, offers retrieval practice, and provides opportunities for feedback.

Surface learning happens best when teachers employ specific, high-impact approaches that foster initial acquisition of content understand-ing, followed by associated procedural skills to then consolidate this learning. We will first guide you in the selection of science learning tasks that promote surface learning, building on our example with Ms. Cross. These include the following:

- Activating and integrating prior knowledge
- Scientific explanation
- Vocabulary instruction
- Imagery and visuals
- Mnemonics

We will also discuss surface learning through the processes of science. These include

- Observing
- Classifying and sequencing
- Communicating

- Measuring
- Predicting
- Hypothesizing
- Inferring
- Using variables in experiments
- Designing, constructing, and interpreting models
- Interpreting, analyzing, and evaluating data

Keep in mind that the goal during the surface phase of learning is to create sufficient time and space for students to acquire and consolidate knowledge, with an eye toward moving on to deepen their understanding. You should not stay in this phase longer than you need to, but neither should you rush through it and leave learners behind. Our mantra is "as fast as we can, as slow as we must." Two important reminders are key to visible learning for science:

1. The teacher clearly signals the learning intentions and success criteria to ensure that students know what they are learning, why they are learning it, and how they will know they have learned it. This clarity should guide all instructional decisions, but, as Ms. Cross demonstrated, the purpose does not have to be revealed at the outset of every lesson.

2. The teacher does not hold any instructional strategy in higher esteem than his or her students' learning. Visible learning is a continual evaluation of one's impact on students. When the evidence suggests that learning has not occurred, the instruction needs to change (not the child!). This is not a specific strategy but a location in the learning process.

Selecting Science Tasks That Promote Surface Learning

For learners to engage in science at a deep level and then apply concepts, ideas, and scientific processes to new contexts (i.e., transfer), they must have a strong enough foundation through a conceptual understanding of scientific practices, crosscutting concepts, and disciplinary core ideas. As we discussed previously, effective progression through the learning process requires that teachers select the right task at the right time, based on the learning intention and success criteria. The task should provide opportunities for students to make meaning of the scientific ideas and processes by allowing the students to experience or create multiple representations of the content, explore and identify patterns in the content, and, at the same time, be contextualized so that the learning is relevant and authentic (Medina, 2014).

The Structure of Observed Learning Outcome (SOLO) Taxonomy (Biggs & Collis, 1982) provides a framework for considering what is and is not surface learning, therefore providing clarity in our learning intentions, success criteria, and selection of tasks. Surface learning is primarily at the uni-structural and multi-structural level. Consider Table 2.2, which shows the uni-structural and multi-structural levels for learners who are developing surface learning about matter and energy in organisms and ecosystems (NGSS Lead States, 2013).

Video 2.2
The SOLO Taxonomy

*http://resources.corwin
.com/vl-science*

For the uni-structural level of thinking, learners are expected to focus on a single idea—in this case, food—and how the availability of food influences predators in an ecosystem. The focus is on developing the initial learning necessary for understanding relationships between organisms and ecosystems. For the multi-level structure of thinking, learners are expected to add additional variables or complexity to their learning by developing the conceptual understanding that organisms interact within ecosystems across multiple variables. The focus is not the single idea of food availability but rather multiple resources in an ecosystem.

Through clear and explicit learning intentions and success criteria, teachers can better select the tasks for this initial learning. The tasks should not be limited to rote memorization but should provide the right amount of rigor and challenge for conceptual understanding. By *rigor*, of course, we are referring to the balance between difficulty and complexity. For this phase of the learning process, tasks tend to be of low difficulty and of low to moderate complexity. This does not prevent teachers from adjusting the level of difficulty or complexity to provide the right amount of challenge to their learners.

For example, we could make the panther hunt less difficult by reducing the number of organisms in the classroom ecosystem, confining the hunting area or ecosystem to a group's table, placing images on the cups rather than single letters, or including the translated name of each animal for those students whose native language is not English. In each of

SOLO Level	Learning Intention	Success Criteria
Uni-structural	I understand that food availability influences other organisms in an ecosystem.	I can identify examples of how food availability influences a predator in an ecosystem.
Multi-structural	I understand that abundant and scare resources influence the population and growth of organisms in an ecosystem.	I can describe how populations of organisms depend on interactions with other living things. I can explain that competition for resources, such as food, constrains population growth.

Table 2.2

the previous examples, the change in the activity reduces the amount of effort required by learners without adjusting the complexity or level of thinking. This would adjust the task so that learners with less background knowledge, those with a disability, or English language learners would have the same access and opportunity to meet the learning intention and success criteria. Likewise, we could increase the difficulty by adding additional organisms, including organisms that are not prey to panthers, or by imposing limitations on panthers (e.g., a broken leg or blindness).

To increase the level of thinking, or complexity, for this task, learners might be required to document evidence to support their descriptions and explanations of these interactions and constraints. What is worth noting here is that as learners become successful at specific levels of complexity, they are ready to move to the next phase of their learning. This is what is meant by not staying in the surface phase longer than you need to, but at the same time not rushing through it and leaving learners behind. Again, the mantra is "as fast as we can, as slow as we must." Increasing the complexity of the panther hunt begins the transition to deeper learning, and at this point, the timing may not be right.

Surface Learning in Science Made Visible

To make surface learning visible in the science classroom, teachers must use the right strategy at the right time. We will next explore the following high-impact instructional strategies for surface learning:

- Activating and integrating prior knowledge
- Scientific explanation
- Vocabulary instruction
- Imagery and visuals
- Mnemonics

Activating and Integrating Prior Knowledge

The role of prior knowledge cannot be overemphasized in the science classroom.

Prior knowledge can be described as the essential knowledge, skills, understandings, and key experiences needed in order to successfully engage in new learning. What experiences students have or what they already know about the content is one of the strongest predictors of how well they will assimilate the new information (Hattie, 2012). These prior experiences are one part of the interaction between the processing and storing of information and experiences in the science classroom (Bransford, Brown, & Cocking, 2000; National Research Council, 2007).

> Effect size for prior knowledge and achievement = 0.67

Making surface learning visible allows teachers to monitor and adjust the learning process based on student thinking. Examples include entrance tickets, exit tickets, brainstorming, and concept mapping. An essential component of the learning process involves both the teacher and the student actively and continuously monitoring student learning through specific strategies designed to make student thinking visible. These strategies should encourage students to think about ideas.

Steven Patterson is introducing the conservation of mass to his sixth graders. Over the next several lessons, learners will develop an understanding that regardless of the types of changes in matter, the total mass of matter is conserved. Given the abstract nature of this topic, the conversation of mass, Mr. Patterson has provided his learners with a task that will elicit prior knowledge. He has provided the following clear and explicit success criteria: (1) I can determine whether mass is conserved in a closed system, and (2) I can identify evidence to support whether mass is conserved in a closed system.

At the students' lab benches, there are two sets of supplies and equipment, along with two slips of paper containing two scenarios. Mr. Patterson asks his learners to find their science interactive notebooks and turn to the next available blank right-hand page. His students quickly glue the two slips of paper containing the scenarios onto the right side of their interactive notebooks. Mr. Patterson then asks his learners to consider the different scenarios. He describes both scenarios to the students, pointing out each piece of equipment and supplies.

> *Scenario #1: On your laboratory bench, there is a small beaker with 250 mL of water and a second beaker with 25 g of salt. Before I do anything, I am going to mass the beaker of water. If I pour the salt into the beaker of water and stir with the stirring rod, will the reading on the scale go up, go down, or stay the same?*

> *Scenario #2: The second setup on the laboratory bench has a small beaker with 250 mL of water and four Alka-Seltzer tablets. Before I do anything, I am going to mass the beaker of water and the Alka-Seltzer tables. If I put the tablets into the beaker of water and stir with the stirring rod, will the reading on the scale go up, go down, or stay the same?*

Mr. Patterson asks his learners to use the left side of the interactive notebooks to first make a prediction and then explain their thinking. After his students have had an opportunity to make a prediction for each scenario and explain their thinking, Mr. Patterson provides time for learners to discuss their ideas with their neighbors. During this process, Mr. Patterson is moving about the room, looking at students' predictions and explanations and listening to their discussions. Prior to allowing students to test their predictions for each scenario, he invites questions from students, recording them on poster paper for later discussion.

The information generated by Mr. Patterson's strategies (e.g., clarity of learning intention and success criteria, classroom discussion, self-questioning, meta-cognition, cooperative learning, small-group learning, writing, and activating prior knowledge) are tools that make thinking and learning visible, giving both Mr. Patterson and his learners feedback about where to go next in the learning process. When learning is visible to both the students and the teacher, all members of the classroom are aware of what they have brought to the learning experience and what initial learning of concepts and skills is needed to progress through the learning process. Our options are (1) to build background knowledge or surface knowledge that is missing, but needed for deeper learning; (2) to activate prior knowledge or surface knowledge, bringing prior experiences to conscious awareness; or (3) to use a combination of these two approaches.

Effect size for self-questioning = 0.64

Effect size for meta-cognitive strategies = 0.69

Scientific Explanation

If surface learning is the initiation of new ideas that begins with the development of conceptual understanding and then the introduction of labels and procedures to give structure to the concepts (Hattie, Fisher, & Frey, 2017), then learners must have multiple opportunities to make meaning of the concepts so that the labels and procedures do provide structure instead of rote memorization of terms. As we mentioned previously, meaning-making involves experiencing or creating multiple representations of the content, exploring and identifying patterns in the content, and, at the same time, providing context so that the learning is relevant and authentic (Medina, 2014). When learners construct scientific explanations, or the discussion of scientific ideas, they actively exchange representations of scientific concepts, make their thinking visible so that they can recognize patterns, and emotionally connect with the ideas by sharing their own perspectives on scientific phenomena (Cazden, 2001; Duschl & Osborne, 2002). The more opportunities learners have to construct scientific explanations and engage in the discussion of scientific ideas, the greater the learning of science concepts (Newton, Driver, & Osborne, 1999; Zembal-Saul, McNeill, & Hershberger, 2012).

Effect size for classroom discussion = 0.82

Zembal-Saul and colleagues (2012) developed the Claim-Evidence-Reason-Rebuttal (CERR) framework for supporting explanation in the science classroom. According to this framework, learners are first asked to make a claim or provide an answer to a scientific question: For example, "Is it an insect?" (see Figure 2.5).

SAMPLE SCIENTIFIC QUESTION: "IS IT AN INSECT?"

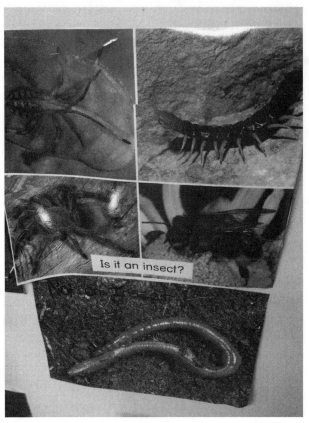

Image courtesy of Orange County Public Schools

Figure 2.5

Young learners must answer the question or make a statement that addresses the question or problem. In this case, a learner might say that the earthworm is not an insect. To foster scientific explanation, the teacher prompts the student to provide evidence supporting his or her claim. This requires the student to cognitively construct his or her conceptual understanding of an insect and verbalize that to his or her peers.

The student must then give a reason why the stated evidence is indeed evidence. Finally, other learners in the classroom are invited to describe or provide a rebuttal, or alternative perspective, and engage in the CERR framework as well. This process increases conceptual understanding of initial ideas by

1. Requiring students to describe concepts instead of regurgitating a definition

2. Asking students to identify relevant evidence and use it to support a claim. This involves asking students to support their claims by explicitly asking, "What makes you say that?"

3. Offering multiple opportunities for students to make explicit connections between ideas

4. Providing students with opportunities to explore the data and, on their own, extract foundational knowledge

5. Providing multiple exposures, through different lenses, and from different perspectives (Ritchhart, Church, & Morrison, 2011)

There are several strategies that embed explaining into the science classroom and also integrate literacy skills into science learning. Paired questioning, the jigsaw, and the jigsaw with partners are three examples that we will explore further.

Paired Questioning

For paired questioning (Manzo, 1969), learners are assigned a partner, and both students are given selection of a text that is grade-level appropriate. For example, a text on simple machines, work, and forces that aligns with grade-level content standards and is complex enough to require a collaborative conversation would work. Both students in each pair read the title and/or the subheadings of the text (nonfictional text, a chapter, or, in most cases, a section of a chapter). Then the students close their books. Each student in turn asks any question he or she wishes related to the title or subheadings. The other student responds and supports his or her claim with evidence and reasoning. These questions should focus on predicting what the students will be learning, how it relates to the learning intention and success criteria, and/or what the text will not address with regard to the day's learning. Example questions could include the following:

> Effect size for literacy through science = 0.98

"How do you think this reading will help our learning today?"

"Can you identify possible ideas that will be discussed in this reading?"

"What part of the learning intention and success criteria will this reading address?"

After these initial predictions are discussed, the students read the selection silently. After completion of the reading, one student asks his or her partner a question from the reading. Again, the other student responds (with a claim), supports his or her response with evidence, and then shares his or her reasoning using specific sections, sentences, or quotes from the text. After responding, this student now gets to ask a question, requiring the other student to engage in the process. This continues until the teacher is ready to move to the next phase.

One of the students must then state what he or she believes to be the important ideas in the selection, as well as what he or she believes to be the unimportant ideas. The student should be encouraged to relate this to the learning intention and success criteria for the day. The other partner must either agree or disagree and give his or her reasons. As an exit activity, each student should write a paraphrase or summary of the selection in his or her interactive notebook. Partners may read their paraphrases to each other and prepare a synopsis that they both agree accurately summarizes the passage and how the reading addresses the learning intention and success criteria.

To scaffold this process for younger learners or learners with different levels of readiness or proficiency with reading, teachers can provide predetermined questions or question sheets for each pair. Furthermore, this activity can be differentiated by providing the content through different modalities—for example, translated into Spanish or another language, presented as an audiovisual file, or supported with a graphic organizer to assist with the reading process. Again, this would give all students access to scientific explanation.

Jigsaw

The jigsaw is a popular approach that can be used to

1. Reinforce students' initial learning experience with new content

2. Provide initial instruction on a concept

3. Motivate somewhat reluctant learners to become involved in the learning process

4. Help students master surface learning that may be difficult for them to master alone

5. Assist teachers in working with learners with different levels of prior knowledge

6. Develop students' fluency with concepts needed for deeper learning

In a jigsaw, content is first divided into four content parts. For example, a high school earth science teacher might focus on the way stars produce elements, and the four content parts chosen are nucleosynthesis, mass of the star, location in the life cycle of a star, and different elements. In step one of the jigsaw, the teacher then assigns one part to each member of a four-person group. In step two, once each member has had time to review his or her part independently, he or she will gather with other members of the class who also have been assigned that part of the jigsaw. For example, in a class of 24, there would be six students assigned to the component of the jigsaw related to the mass of the star. This expert group develops a teaching strategy for helping their original groups "learn" the content. After some time, the experts return to their home groups, and in step three, they teach their fellow classmates their specific part of the content. Finally, in step four, students return to their expert teams and discuss with their peers how their component fits with the other components. For example, the expert group focused on nucleosynthesis will discuss that topic in relation to the other three topics they learned about during the home group discussions.

> Effect size for jigsaw = 1.20

> Effect size for microteaching = 0.88

The order of the student-led instruction could be determined by the students or preset by the teacher. To determine whether students have developed the necessary conceptual understanding needed for deeper learning, teachers should provide a formative assessment that provides feedback on where to go next in the learning process.

The jigsaw strategy could be modified to work with partners as well. For this modification, the content is divided up into two parts: for example, chemical changes and physical changes. Learners would be assigned one of the two possible topics and would have some time to review the material alone. Then students would consult with their same-topic peers to devise a teaching strategy for either chemical or physical changes. After some time, the subject experts would go back and teach their assigned partners the content.

As with paired questioning, to scaffold the jigsaw process for younger learners or learners with different levels of readiness, teachers can provide predetermined approaches for teaching content. Furthermore, this activity can also be differentiated by providing the content through different modalities—for example, translated into Spanish or another language, presented as an audiovisual file, or supported with a graphic organizer to assist with the expert learning process.

There are a number of strategies that provide learners with opportunities to engage in scientific explanation. We have focused on just three of those strategies. Any strategy you pick to increase scientific explanation should engage learners in relevant tasks that support their initial learning of concepts in science. The paired questioning, jigsaw, and jigsaw with partners strategies all allow learners to construct scientific explanations, engage in the discussion of scientific ideas, actively exchange representations of scientific concepts, make their thinking visible so that they can recognize patterns, and emotionally connect with the ideas by sharing their own perspectives on scientific phenomena (Cazden, 2001; Duschl & Osborne, 2002).

Vocabulary Instruction

Effect size for vocabulary instruction = 0.67

In science, teachers recognize the importance and necessity of students' being very comfortable with the scientific terminology or vocabulary required for learning in the classroom. For example, the difference between speed and velocity is significant in developing a conceptual understanding of two-dimensional and three-dimensional motion. In biology and chemistry, learners must be fluent with the language of chemical reactions: cations, anions, and valence electrons. These terms are foundational and thus are integral to the surface learning of students. Having students memorize the definition of each term by first copying the definition into their notebooks and then studying the terms is not the solution. If students do not have experiences to make meaning of the terminology in the text, they may not do anything beyond copying the definition, or what we call the "assign-define-test" approach to word learning.

Prior knowledge often manifests itself as vocabulary knowledge. If students have word knowledge, they are very likely to have conceptual and background knowledge. Thus, the academic vocabulary knowledge of our science students is strongly associated with the breadth and depth of their background knowledge (Marzano, 2004; Marzano & Pickering, 2005). Research evidence suggests that the process of building academic background knowledge should include direct vocabulary instruction (Hattie, 2009, 2012; Marzano, 2004). This direct vocabulary instruction should require students to (1) develop descriptions of words, rather than just definitions; (2) incorporate both linguistic and nonlinguistic representations; (3) include multiple exposures to the words or concepts; (4) encourage students to discuss the words or concepts; (5) require students to play with words; and (6) focus on words that are necessary for academic success (Marzano, 2004; Marzano & Pickering, 2005). Learners should have a conceptual understanding of the concepts and terms within their unit of study.

One of the many ways to encourage students to play with concepts, terms, and vocabulary is with a word wall. Select an area of your classroom and designate that area as the word wall for a particular unit or topic, even with middle and high school students. There are a couple of variations on this strategy that vary according to the amount of teacher involvement. One approach is for you, the teacher, to scatter the concepts, terms, or vocabulary all over the word wall. A second option would be to have students participate in a pre-reading or brainstorming activity where the students generate a list of concepts, terms, or vocabulary for the wall, as demonstrated in the following example:

Teacher: *Good morning! To start class today, you will need your textbook, a sheet of paper, and something to write with.*

The teacher pauses and waits for the students to gather their materials.

Teacher: *Great. Please check with your neighbors and make sure they have their textbook, a sheet of paper, and something to write with. If they do, give me a thumbs-up. If not, please help them out.*

The teacher pauses and waits for the students to give the thumbs-up signal.

Teacher: *Please find page 105 in your resource book, the first page of the chapter on plant structure and growth. When you are there, give me a thumbs-up.*

The teacher pauses and waits for the students to give the thumbs-up signal.

Teacher: *Please look through the chapter and make a list of 10 to 15 concepts, terms, or words that you think are important in the chapter. See if you can get 10 to 15 on your list in 2 minutes. Go!*

Regardless of whether you use a teacher-generated list or a student-generated list, these words should be scattered on the word wall for students to see and use in context every day. For example, you might have students pick two or three words and explain their meaning to a neighbor. Students might be asked to select one or two words and create a visual sketch of the terms. As an exit activity, students might pick the concepts, terms, or vocabulary from the day's lesson and create a few sentences that conceptually link the words together. The key is to have your students interact with each other and the words on a regular basis.

To ensure multiple exposures and representations of the concepts, terms, and vocabulary necessary for academic success, students can create a chart on which they write a description of the word ("Write It"), draw a visual representation of the word ("Draw It"), and then provide a concrete example ("Apply It"; see Figure 2.6).

Imagery and Visuals

In science, teachers cannot always bring the real thing into the classroom. For example, nuclear fusion, the weather on Jupiter, or cellular respiration and the Krebs cycle would be impossible to demonstrate as a lab. To provide students with a concrete experience that facilitates their conceptual understanding, teachers must develop alternate representations of these scientific phenomena that include text, pictures, gestures, animations, demonstrations, models, analogies, and metaphors. These alternate and external representations allow teachers to provide a secondhand experience of concepts when direct experience is limited due to safety, emotional impact, accessibility, or clarity. These representations aim to develop student understanding by supporting the structure and development of their internal representations. For surface learning, text and pictures are most effective (Treagust & Tsui, 2014).

For example, to help learners understand the process by which blood passes into and out of the heart, a teacher could choose to provide a written description and deliver this content through notes, through a fill-in-the-blank handout, or simply by telling his or her students how the process works. Given the complexity of this content and how foundational this content is to understanding other physiological processes of the body (respiration, the vascular system, blood pressure,

SAMPLE CHART: WRITE IT, DRAW IT/APPLY IT

Concept, Term, or Vocabulary	Write It (Description)	Draw It /Apply It
Parallel circuit	Two or more coplanar lines that have no points in common	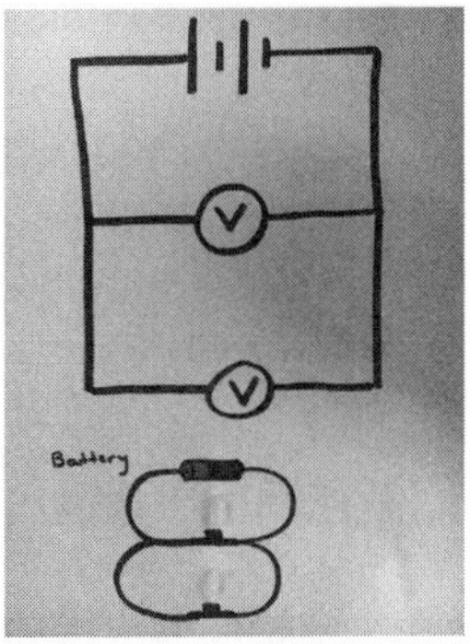
Centrifugal force	A force that keeps a body moving with a uniform speed along a circular path and is directed along the radius toward the center.	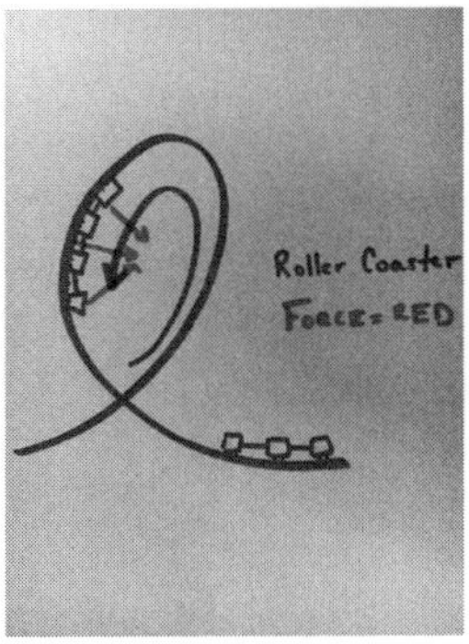

Figure 2.6

cholesterol, blood cells, blood cell count, etc.), students must have a conceptual understanding developed through a meaning-making task. Research in science education, as well as the science of learning, strongly suggests that the use of visuals facilitates learning (Hattie & Yates, 2014; Mayer, 2003, 2011). Furthermore, research suggests that visuals used with words may provide an ideal combination as an alternate or external representation. Mayer (2003, 2011), through incredible research on how we encode information, identified specific principles to guide representations that involve words and images:

1. Listening to and reading the same information is not efficient and will reduce our overall learning (Sweller, 2005). This is redundant. The solution is to either listen or read, but not both.

2. We learn better when words are placed as close to relevant images as possible. This is known as *contiguity* (Mayer, 2005). Figure 2.7 presents an example of this principle. Which diagram is easier to process: the one on the right or the one on the left?

3. *Multimedia principle:* We learn better from words and pictures than from words alone (Fletcher & Tobias, 2005). Our minds efficiently combine words and images (see Figure 2.8 for examples of words only versus words paired with visuals).

4. We need to see how knowledge applies to specific cases through *worked examples* (Hattie & Yates, 2014; see Figure 2.9).

5. We benefit from *signaling*, or any cues that highlight critical information (Mayer, 2005; see Figure 2.10).

When supporting learning in the initial phase of the learning process, provide alternate or external representations that allow students to make meaning of abstract concepts.

Mnemonics

Mnemonics are memory devices that assist learners in recalling substantial amounts of information, including science concepts such as the visible part of the electromagnetic spectrum, the order of the planets, or the direction of the torque in rotational motion. "It is a memory enhancing instructional strategy which involves teaching students to link new information that is taught to information they already know" (DeLashmutt, 2007, p. 1). As is often the case, mnemonics could be a short song, an acronym, or a visual image that is easily remembered to help students who have difficulty recalling information.

How often have you used this strategy (even if you could not name it) to recall a string of words? "ROY G. BIV" is often used to remember the colors of the light spectrum (red, orange, yellow, green, blue, indigo, and violet), or "HOMES" is used to recall the names of the U.S. Great Lakes (Huron, Ontario, Michigan, Erie, and Superior). In addition to acronyms and musical mnemonics, other techniques include using an image or an expression (e.g., "Every Good Boy Does Fine" to recall that the lines on the musical treble staff are E, G, B, D, and F).

EXAMPLE OF CONTIGUITY

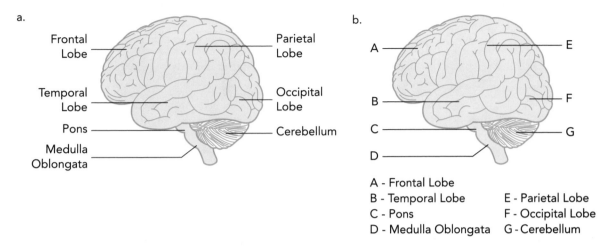

Source: Dr. Gregory M. Francom, Associate Professor of E-Learning, Northern State University

Figure 2.7

Mnemonics are especially helpful with the vocabulary of science. For example, the layers of the atmosphere are recalled by reciting the phrase "The Strong Man's Triceps Explode" to represent troposphere, stratosphere, mesosphere, thermosphere, and exosphere. "Sir Can Rig A VCR, PA!" is used to represent the brightest stars in the sky: *Sirius, Canopus, Rigil Kent, Acrturus, Vega, Capella, Rigel, Procyon,* and *Achernar*. As another example, "Limping Dreadfully, King Phillip Came Over From Great Spain" stands for life, domain, kingdom, phylum, class, order, family, genus, and species. These mnemonics do not replace an understanding of each layer of the atmosphere, the relative brightness of stars, or the system for biological classification; they simply help students place the labels correctly as they work with the terms.

Another challenging set of terms in science is the prefixes of the metric system. One common device for helping learners sequence them correctly is "King Henry Doesn't Usually Drink Cold Milk"; the first initials of this sentence correspond to the prefixes kilo-, hecto-, deca-, unit, deci-, centi-, and milli-. Students must still know the prefixes and how they correspond to the scale of a unit. In addition, they have to

EXAMPLE OF THE MULTIMEDIA PRINCIPLE

a.

Stages of Mitosis

1. In prophase, the chromosomes start to condense, the mitotic spindle begins to form, and the nucleolus disappears.

2. In metaphase, all of the chromosomes align at the metaphase plate, and the two kinetochores of each chromosome are attached to the microtubules.

3. In anaphase, the chromatids separate, and the cell becomes longer.

4. In telophase, the mitotic spindle is broken, two new nuclei form, nuclear membranes and nucleoli form, and chromosomes decondense.

5. In cytokinesis, the cytoplasm divides to form two new cells.

b.

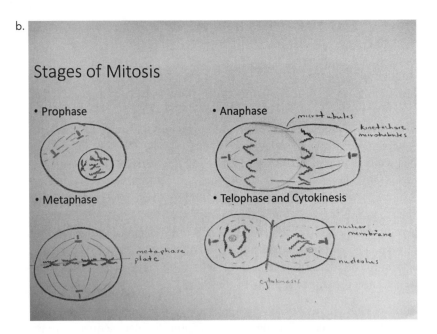

Figure 2.8

WORKED EXAMPLE

If y is proportional to the square of x:

a. If $y = 120$ when $x = 4$, find a formula for y in terms of x.

$$y = kx^2$$
$$120 = k(4)^2$$
$$120 = k(16)$$

So, $k = \dfrac{120}{16}$

$k = \dfrac{30}{4} = \dfrac{15}{2}$

$\boxed{y = \dfrac{15}{2} x^2}$

b. Find y when $x = 7.5$.

plug into formula from (a).

$$y = \dfrac{15}{2}(7.5)^2 = \dfrac{15}{2}(56.25) = \boxed{421.9}$$

c. Find the value of x for which $y = 125$.

$$y = kx^2$$
$$y = \dfrac{15}{2}x^2$$
$$y = 125$$

So, $125 = \dfrac{15}{2}x^2$

$250 = 15x^2$

$16.7 = x^2$

$x = \sqrt{16.7}$

$\boxed{x = 4.09}$

Figure 2.9

distinguish between the two "d" prefixes (deca-, or 10 times, and deci-, or one-tenth). Using understanding (i.e., decimals involve units smaller than 1) rather than depending on memorization makes sense and therefore makes it more likely for students to remember the distinction.

Mnemonics can be useful if used appropriately. Too often, they are used not to reduce storage in working memory to use the ideas in problem solving, but to replace an understanding or to present students with a trick that overrides an important understanding, which often leads to misconceptions (Karp, Bush, & Dougherty, 2014). Thus, it is important to ensure that students understand the reasoning behind the mnemonics and not just the procedures for using them. Mnemonics work to get students to surface-level understanding, but we cannot leave them there. As Jeon (2012) notes, simply memorizing the order of the visible part of the electromagnetic spectrum does not mean that

Video 2.3
Making Science Surface
Learning Visible

*http://resources.corwin
.com/vl-science*

73

Reduction—Oxidation Reactions

- **Oxidation States Are Changed**
  - ○ **Redox** reactions include all chemical reactions in which atoms have their oxidation state changed.
- **Reduction Is Gain**
  - ○ The **gain** of electrons is **reduction** and results in a decrease in the oxidation in the oxidation state of the molecule, atom, or ion.
- **Oxidation Is Loss**
  - ○ The **loss** of electrons is **oxidation** and results in an increase in the oxidation state of molecule, atom, or ion.

Figure 2.10

students know how to use the information or understand the concepts of frequency and wavelength.

Scientific Processes and Thinking

Science is a body of knowledge, a specific way of knowing, and a set of processes. Science is not merely a list of facts about frogs, planets, and the human body. Instead, science is the complex interaction among theories, principles, and natural laws, the unique nature of science, and scientific thinking. Thus, the learning process for science involves a strong foundation in this body of knowledge as well as the processes that have supported and refuted that body of knowledge. Klahr, Zimmerman, and Jirout (2011) state that "scientific thinking can be characterized in terms of two principle features: (1) content, which includes an array of domain-specific topics, such as physics, chemistry, biology, Earth sciences, and so on . . . and (2) processes including formulation of hypotheses, design of experiments, and evaluation of evidence" (p. 971). Put differently, learners engage in a learning progression of the scientific processes just as they do with science content. There is a surface learning phase for the science processes of observing; classifying and sequencing; communicating; measuring; predicting; hypothesizing; inferring; using variables in experiments; designing, constructing, and interpreting models; and interpreting, analyzing, and evaluating data. Let's look more closely at observing now.

PROCESS PROGRESSION
CHART FOR OBSERVING

1. Basic characteristics or properties of objects are identified by direct observation.

2. Observations are made from multiple positions to achieve different perspectives.

3. The senses are used to observe differences in physical properties.

4. Observations are made from multiple positions to achieve a variety of perspectives and are repeated to ensure accuracy.

5. Simple tools are used to enhance observations.

6. Observations and predictions are made, and questions are formed.

7. Observation is differentiated from personal interpretation.

8. Observations are repeated to ensure accuracy.

9. Distinctions are made among observations, conclusions, inferences, and predictions.

10. Observations are made involving fine discriminations between similar objects and organisms.

11. Observations of living things are recorded in the lab and in the field.

12. Instruments are selected and used to extend observations and measurements of mass, volume, temperature, heat exchange, energy transformations, motion, fields, and electric charge. (adapted from VDOE, 2012)

SOLO TAXONOMY LEVELS: SURFACE LEARNING OF SCIENTIFIC PROCESSES AND THINKING

SOLO Level	Learning Intention	Success Criteria
Uni-structural	I understand that the characteristics of objects are identified by direct observation.	I can identify the properties of an object by using my senses.
Multi-structural	I understand that observations can be made from multiple perspectives.	I can describe an object from different positions. I can identify differences in an object from different perspectives.

Table 2.3

The SOLO Taxonomy mentioned previously (Biggs & Collis, 1982) provides a framework for considering what is and is not surface learning of content; similarly, the taxonomy also provides guidance on the progression of learning for the processes of science. The appropriate level of challenge is to have each learner at the right level of the SOLO Taxonomy for content and the right level of the SOLO for scientific thinking. Surface learning of scientific processes and thinking happens primarily at the uni-structural and multi-structural levels (see Table 2.3).

For the uni-structural level of thinking, learners are expected to focus on an object from a single perspective. The focus is on developing the initial learning necessary for observing objects and identifying basic characteristics and properties. For the multi-level structure of thinking, learners are expected to add multiple perspectives by observing an object from multiple positions.

Beginning in kindergarten, students make progress in learning how to think like a scientist and engage in the processes of science. Asking learners to engage in scientific thinking before they have the foundational knowledge to do so will hamper the learning process and will

EFFECTIVE FEEDBACK CHART

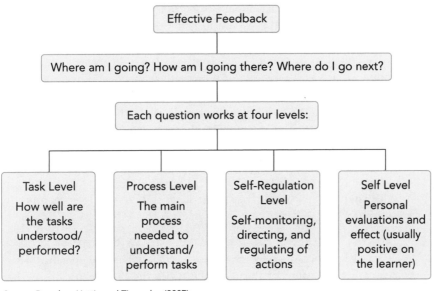

Source: Based on Hattie and Timperley (2007).

Figure 2.11

likely lead to frustration and disengagement for both the teacher and the students.

Feedback

In Chapter 1, we described effective feedback as information exchanged between the teacher and student, or between the student and his or her peers, that answers three questions: (1) Where am I going? (2) How am I going there? and (3) Where do I go next? This can be done by offering learners task feedback, providing them with process feedback, or engaging them in self-regulation feedback (see Figure 2.11). Praise feedback is not strongly associated with learning; thus, we will not focus on this fourth type of feedback.

Notice that in Figure 2.11, for the surface stage of the learning process, task feedback is very important as learners begin to test and conceptualize the abstract boundaries of specific science content, ideas, and terms—for example, the specific differences between a predator and prey or situations where an animal is sometimes a predator and sometimes prey, depending on the circumstances. Learners rely on task feedback to add structure to the concept of what is and is not an example and in what context. For example, this feedback should help the learner determine what is and what is not a predator or prey. Another example is the conceptual boundary between a closed system and an open system with regard to the conservation of mass. As learners struggle with the difference between an open and a closed system, they will need examples and non-examples of each type of system. Task feedback provides clear information to the learner that sorts out relevant and essential features of these two ideas. This applies to each of the content examples in this chapter (i.e., simple machines, stars, and chemical versus physical changes).

Effective feedback is characterized not only by the type of feedback (i.e., task, process, or self-regulation), but also by the specificity and constructive nature of the feedback. Does the teacher use his or her learners' explanations, conversations during the jigsaw activity, interactions during paired questioning, and their representations of content as feedback on their learning? This feedback to the teacher should inform the type and nature of the feedback given to his or her learners. Each student's successful assimilation of feedback, and thus using the feedback to decide where to go next, rests solely on whether each learner understands what the feedback means and how he or she can use it to move forward in the learning. Effective feedback and effective use of that feedback supports the consolidation of initial learning and calls for scaffolding through teacher-activated instruction with an explicit introduction to the structure of the content.

As learners begin to develop conceptual understanding and fluency with each of these concepts, the feedback should increasingly regard process. Whether from the teacher or peers, learners should receive feedback on their thinking, not just the accuracy of their response. For example, teachers might engage students in further dialogue about chemical and physical changes: "Remember, a physical change is a reversible change in the physical properties of a substance. What changed in this example?" This feedback does not tell the student that he or she is right or wrong. Instead, the feedback, in the form of a question, asks the student to think about the process by which he or she determined whether something was or was not a physical change.

As learners move through the learning process from surface, to deep, to transfer, the feedback between the teacher and the learner and between the learner and his or her peers should reflect this progression as well.

Conclusion

A strong start sets the stage for meaningful learning and powerful impact. Teachers need to be mindful of where their students are in the learning cycle. Surface learning establishes the necessary foundation for the deepening knowledge and transfer that will come later. But there's a caveat: Teaching for transfer must occur. Too often, learning ends at the surface level. The challenge is this: We can't overcorrect in the other direction, bypassing foundational knowledge in favor of critical and analytic thinking. Students need and deserve to be introduced to new knowledge and skills thoughtfully and with a great deal of expertise on the part of the teacher. And teachers need to recognize the signs that it is time to move forward from surface learning to deep learning.

Reflection Questions

1. Consider the science topics for your grade level. What is the surface learning phase of each topic? What would that look like in the uni- and multi-structural levels of a SOLO chart? What specific strategies might you use to help students develop surface learning for each of these topics?

2. Consider how you structure the learning of foundational knowledge in your classroom. Do you focus on exercises or tasks? How could you take an exercise and modify it into a task that promotes conceptual understanding?

3. How often do your learners have the opportunity to engage in scientific explanations? What opportunities do students have to explain and justify their thinking? What strategies could you use to provide additional opportunities for students to show their learning through explanation and justification?

4. Are your students encouraged to create or develop multiple representations as they learn science content? What strategies can you use to encourage students to find patterns within science content? What tools could you make available to your students to help them make meaning of the content?

SCIENCE DEEP LEARNING MADE VISIBLE

3

If surface learning is the acquisition and consolidation of initial learning within a particular topic and through process skills associated with the topic, deep learning engages learners in uncovering the relationships between terms, concepts, and ideas within that topic. Recalling the example from Chapter 2, as learners begin to develop a conceptual understanding of the conservation of mass, deep learning calls for the scaffolding of student thinking about the relationships between, say, the conservation of mass, the conservation of atoms in physical and chemical processes, and the transfer of energy in designed and natural processes (e.g., the nitrogen cycle, photosynthesis, and how an engine works). Surface learning focuses on conceptual understanding of the conservation of mass, while deep learning calls for learners to understand how this concept is related to other scientific phenomena. The deep learning phase should provide students with multiple opportunities to utilize science process skills to plan, investigate, and elaborate on their initial learning and extract generalizations about the science content. Let's return to a classroom as learners experience visible deep science learning.

Bryan Smith is a high school chemistry teacher who is developing a series of learning activities to scaffold student understanding of the relationship between the arrangement of the periodic table of elements, the relative properties of elements, and atomic structure (NGSS Lead States, 2013). As learners have acquired and consolidated their understanding of concepts such as boiling point, melting point, ionization energy, and electron affinity, Mr. Smith intends for his learners to uncover the relationship between these concepts, the arrangement of the periodic table of elements, and the atomic structure of atoms. During class, learners will analyze data to develop a mathematical model that illustrates relationships between the previously mentioned ideas and will make generalizations about the periodic table.

Pre-assessment data from yesterday's exit ticket let Mr. Smith know that learners have a conceptual understanding of boiling point, melting point, ionization energy, and electron affinity. Although some of his students are still consolidating this learning, they are able to engage with these concepts through more complex tasks. That is, the pre-assessment made the learning progression of the students visible to both the students and Mr. Smith. Learners are able to elaborate on ($ES = 0.75$) or make connections between the concepts and the atomic structure and arrangement of the periodic table. As students file into the chemistry classroom, they notice the learning intention displayed on the board:

"Today we will understand the relationship between how the periodic table of elements is arranged and the properties of specific elements." Right below the learning intention are the success criteria that the students have grown accustomed to seeing on a daily basis. After all, this is how their learning, and success, is made visible in Mr. Smith's classroom: "I know I understand this relationship when (1) I can graphically represent data from the periodic table of elements on the specific properties of atoms, (2) I can develop a mathematical model that illustrates the relationship between the periodic table and atomic properties, and (3) I can use my model to explain these relationships."

As students enter the classroom, they find a sticky note at each of their seats, next to their laptops. Mr. Smith's classroom is a one-to-one classroom. The number on the sticky note, ranging from 1 to 7, indicates each student's expert group. Mr. Smith informs his learners that they are to change seats and sit with those who have the same number on their sticky note (i.e., all the ones are sitting together, all the twos are sitting together, etc.). Once students have relocated to their expert groups, Mr. Smith provides instructions about the specific task assigned to each group. He informs them that each group will get a question that they must answer and then will use a graphic organizer (see Figure 3.1) that supports the organization of their thinking and findings as they work to answer the question. Each member of the group must have his or her own response, because the students will have to present their findings to their home group. The questions, he tells them, "will contribute to our progress toward today's learning intention."

Mr. Smith distributes folders that contain a brief set of instructions, the graphic organizer, and one of the following questions:

1. Is the boiling point of an element a periodic property?
2. Is the melting point of an element a periodic property?
3. Is atomic mass a periodic property?
4. Is atomic radius a periodic property?
5. Is ionic radius a periodic property?
6. Is the ionization energy of an atom a periodic property?
7. Is the electron affinity of an atom a periodic property?

As a quick note, the number of questions Mr. Smith uses depends on the group size he believes is best for this particular learning experience.

SAMPLE GRAPHIC ORGANIZER

Question:

Claim:

Evidence:	Reason of the Evidence:

Figure 3.1

Specifically, for Mr. Smith's smaller classes, he would prioritize the questions to ensure that the essential understanding is addressed by this activity, eliminating some of the questions (i.e., he may need only five questions to keep group size down). For larger classes, he may use all seven questions or incorporate additional questions relating nuclear charge and shielding to the periodic table of elements to keep group size down. In addition, Mr. Smith could have used student choice. Allowing student groups to choose how they want to answer the learning intention for the day would offer them a choice in their learning experience. Again, this would depend on the characteristics of the class and where they are in their own learning journey.

The instructions state that each team is to graphically and mathematically represent data that would help the group answer the question, as well as provide evidence of that answer. The reason, or justification of the evidence, must be from their chemistry textbook or a professional source, something other than Wikipedia. Mr. Smith turns his learners loose, and they are provided with time to engage in the task, answer their question, and organize their evidence and reasons.

As Mr. Smith moves around the room, listening to student conversations, responding to questions, redirecting learners, and asking probing questions, he promotes elaborate integration ($ES = 0.42$) of content knowledge and process skills. He is also aware when groups are ready to move on to the next step in this learning activity. He instructs the learners to gather their work supplies and regroup. Each group must have a

SAMPLE STUDENT WORK

a.

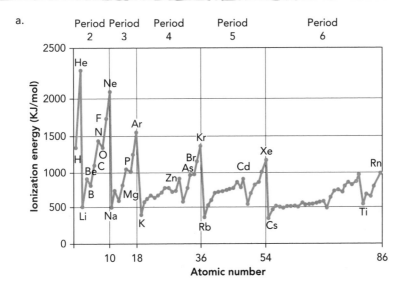

b.

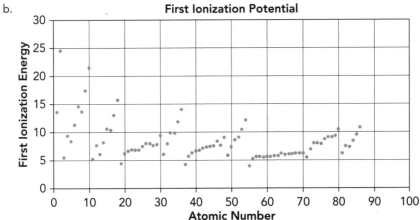

Source: Graphs created by Leonard C. Klein, Shenandoah Valley Governor's School.

Figure 3.2

1, 2, 3, 4, 5, 6, and 7 represented at the table. These are the learning groups. Once settled into their learning groups, students take turns presenting their questions, making their claims, providing their evidence, and justifying the evidence through references to chemistry sources. Figure 3.2 contains an example of one student's work.

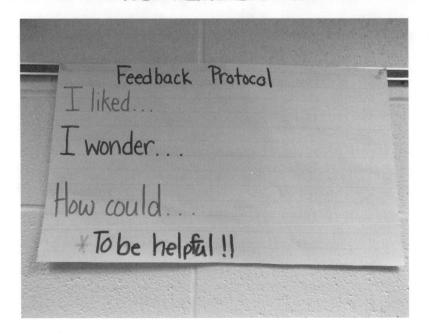

Figure 3.3

As each individual student presents his or her findings, the others in the learning group are taking notes, asking questions, and providing feedback. To support student-driven feedback, something we will address later in this chapter, Mr. Smith has a student-created anchor chart (see Figure 3.3) in the classroom to support this type of dialogue.

To close the lesson, Mr. Smith distributes a periodic table of elements to each student (see Figure 3.4).

He asks his learners to visually represent the periodic properties uncovered during today's learning. In response to his students' unsureness about what he means by "visually represent the periodic properties," Mr. Smith provides a worked example ($ES = 0.57$) showing arrows going down and across the periodic table (see Figure 3.5). "As we move down the rows and across the columns, what happens with each of the periodic properties we explored today?"

This quick example eliminates student uncertainty so that Mr. Smith's learners can continue to consolidate their deep learning. In the space

PERIODIC TABLE OF ELEMENTS

The periodic table of elements shown includes the following:

1	2	3	4	5	6	7	8	9	10	11	12	13	14	15	16	17	18
H																	He
Li	Be											B	C	N	O	F	Ne
Na	Mg											Al	Si	P	S	Cl	Ar
K	Ca	Sc	Ti	V	Cr	Mn	Fe	Co	Ni	Cu	Zn	Ga	Ge	As	Se	Br	Kr
Rb	Sr	Y	Zr	Nb	Mo	Tc	Ru	Rh	Pd	Ag	Cd	In	Sn	Sb	Te	I	Xe
Cs	Ba	57-70 *	Lu	Hf	Ta	W	Re	Os	Ir	Pt	Au	Hg	Tl	Pb	Bi	Po	At	Rn
Fr	Ra	89-102 **	Lr	Rf	Db	Sg	Bh	Hs	Mt	Uun	Uuu	Uub		Uuq				

*Lanthanide series: La (57), Ce (58), Pr (59), Nd (60), Pm (61), Sm (62), Eu (63), Gd (64), Tb (65), Dy (66), Ho (67), Er (68), Tm (69), Yb (70)

**Actinide series: Ac (89), Th (90), Pa (91), U (92), Np (93), Pu (94), Am (95), Cm (96), Bk (97), Cf (98), Es (99), Fm (100), Md (101), No (102)

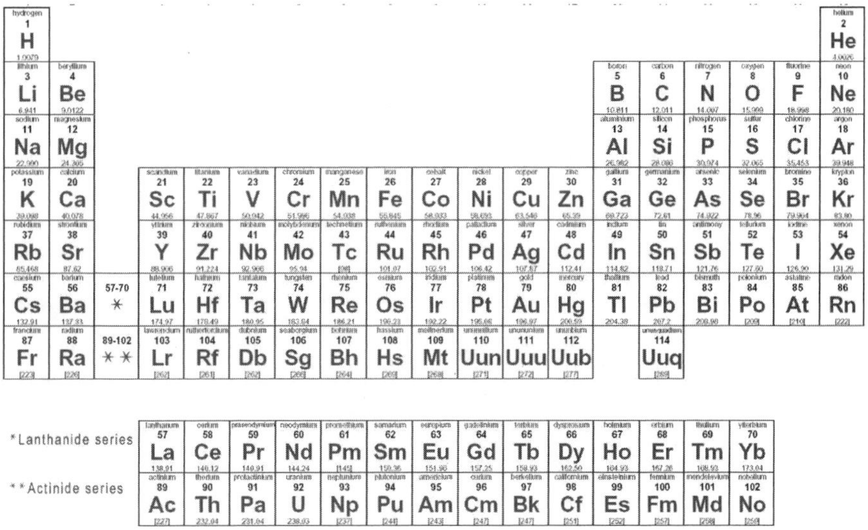

Figure 3.4

provided on the back of the periodic table sheet, he asks the students to provide a self-explanation of today's learning, including those properties that were not periodic: "Explain, in your own words, the properties uncovered today and what you have learned about these properties." This self-explanation ($ES = 0.50$) and reflection ($ES = 0.75$) promote the consolidation of this deeper learning.

Mr. Smith made intentional and purposeful decisions, having evaluated students' previous level of understanding, to provide a learning experience incorporating the elaboration, organizing, and integration of science content knowledge and process skills. This learning experience developed deep learning beyond the initial acquisition of boiling point, melting point, ionization energy, and electron affinity. The learning progression associated with is particular science content and process skills asks students to develop and use models, plan and carry out investigations, and obtain, evaluate, and communicate scientific information related to the structure and properties of matter (NGSS Lead States, 2013). The decisions made by Mr. Smith to engage in this particular learning experience require that his learners have successfully acquired and consolidated the foundational, or surface, knowledge

WORKED EXAMPLE
FOR PERIODIC TABLE

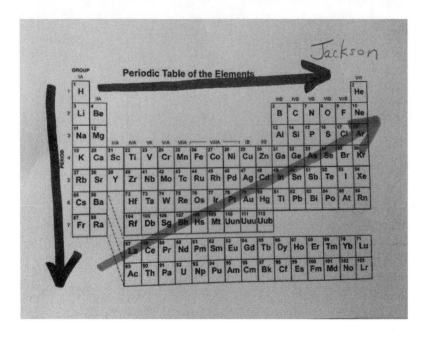

Figure 3.5

and process skills necessary to effectively uncover these relationships within the structure of this content. Only after Mr. Smith has elicited the prior knowledge of his chemistry students, making this background knowledge visible to him and his learners, can he move forward in the learning process with well-timed deep learning experiences. He knew what his students already knew about atomic properties and about the conceptual understanding and vocabulary necessary to develop and use models, plan and carry out investigations, and obtain, evaluate, and communicate scientific information about the relationships between atomic properties and periodic table of elements.

Deep Learning in Science

Deep learning focuses on recognizing relationships among scientific ideas or phenomena. During deep learning, students engage more actively and deliberately with data and evidence in order to discover and understand the underlying scientific principle rather than treating each idea as an independent scientific phenomenon. For example, deep learners move beyond seeing the water cycle, the nitrogen cycle, the rock cycle, and the life cycle of a butterfly as four discrete cycles consisting of steps that are to be memorized. Instead, they extract the cross-cutting concept of change and the relationship between change and external factors that serve as catalysts to this change (i.e., energy). Deep learners are able to make connections and think meta-cognitively—that is, they think about their thinking, discuss ideas, take action, and evaluate evidence as a necessary part of science learning. Thus, deep learners begin to use scientific processes in a more complex way as they seek to uncover these connections.

Remember that this is a cyclical process, and students are constantly moving between surface learning and deep learning. Surface learning is an essential part of the learning process by giving students tasks in which they are building a knowledge base of conceptual understanding that connects to flexible and efficient procedures. This prepares students to engage with more cognitively challenging tasks, and to use more rigorous discourse to identify patterns and make generalizations. For example, as learners engage in answering the question about ionization energy as a periodic property, unexpected gaps in their learning may be visible as they obtain their data and evaluate the evidence supporting their claims. A learner may realize that his or her conceptual understanding of ionization energy is not sufficient to justify the evidence he or she has obtained from the data. The learner, in collaboration with the teacher, may need brief direct or explicit instruction to close that gap so that he or she can continue on in his or her deeper learning. Timing is everything!

Video 3.1
Confirming Learners Are Ready for Deep and Transfer Learning

http://resources.corwin .com/vl-science

Let's revisit the "Teaching for Surface Learning and Teaching for Deeper Learning" chart from the previous chapter (see Table 3.1).

As noted earlier, approaches associated with "teaching for deeper learning" show greater learning gains when used during the deep learning phase (Hattie & Donoghue, 2016; Hattie & Yates, 2014). Comparing Ms. Cross's classroom from Chapter 2 with Mr. Smith's classroom from this chapter, the learning environment is different in the two classrooms. The two main differences are (1) the location of the students in their learning progression and, therefore, (2) the timing of specific approaches or strategies. The learners in Ms. Cross's class were at the surface learning phase and not yet ready to uncover relationships within habitats. Therefore, she purposefully decided to support

Teaching for Surface Learning	Teaching for Deeper Learning
Worked examples, $ES = 0.37$	Student control over learning, $ES = 0.02$
Behavioral organizers, $ES = 0.42$	Web-based learning, $ES = 0.18$
Providing goals, $ES = 0.50$	Problem-based learning, $ES = 0.26$
Mastery learning, $ES = 0.57$	Inquiry-based teaching, $ES = 0.40$
Direct instruction, $ES = 0.60$	Inductive teaching, $ES = 0.44$

Table 3.1

her students' initial learning. On the other hand, Mr. Smith's students demonstrated conceptual understanding of the terms, ideas, and concepts necessary for noticing relationships and forming generalizations. He *deepened* this learning through an inquiry activity. The phase of learning and the timing of approach and strategies matter! We're searching for the right approach, at the right time, for the right type of learning. However, this works the other way as well. What happens when learners have progressed to the deep phase of learning but the learning experiences continue to focus on surface learning? Let's visit Ms. Easton's high school anatomy and physiology class to find out.

Lexi Easton teaches two sections of anatomy and physiology. One of the major and essential understandings in this advanced biology class is that DNA determines the structure of proteins, which carry out essential functions of life through systems of specialized cells. For this group of learners, this includes the identification of specific cell or tissue types, whole-body systems, and the biochemistry of protein synthesis (NGSS Lead States, 2013). The learning intention for this particular unit is "I will understand that DNA determines the structure of proteins and how those proteins carry out the essential functions of life through systems of specialized cells." Although Ms. Easton has presented a lofty learning intention, she has content-task analyzed ($ES = 0.87$) the required knowledge and process skills, breaking down the learning into manageable success criteria. Today the success criteria are (1) "I can explain the hierarchical structural organization of a multicellular organism" and (2) "I can give examples of how this structure supports the essential functions of life" (NGSS Lead States, 2013). From the specific phrasing of the learning intention and the two success criteria, learners are striving to recognize relationships among specific systems of specialized cells and the cells' function in sustaining life. This is deep learning and thus calls for employing specific, high-impact approaches and strategies that foster the uncovering of these relationships.

Ms. Easton decides to have her students develop a set of flash cards to support their learning of the components of systems within multicellular learning. The specific instructions ask students to create flash cards with the structures or components of the circulatory system on the front and their functions on the back (see Figure 3.6).

Ms. Easton makes the same request for the digestive system, the respiratory system, the muscular system, and the nervous system. The idea behind the flash cards is that learners will have multiple opportunities to practice retrieving and recalling the specific functions of components within a multicellular organism. However, consider the approach and strategy selected by Ms. Easton. Think about the timing of this approach and strategy.

Because Ms. Easton's success criteria relate to deep learning, a strategy that facilitates summarizing, organizing, and a form of note-taking may have been better used at a different time in the learning process. Summarizing ($ES = 0.66$), organizing ($ES = 0.60$), and note-taking ($ES = 0.50$) are effective strategies for acquiring surface learning. In other words, the effect size for each of these strategies is associated with initial acquisition of content and not associated with deep learning. Furthermore, the use of flash cards may not provide opportunities for learners to consolidate their learning, resulting in memorization strategies. Just as Ms. Cross effectively assumed her role in developing the surface learning of her students, a classroom teacher can just as easily select approaches or strategies at the wrong time in the learning process. To promote the acquisition and consolidation of deep learning, Ms. Easton may have been better served by engaging her learners in explicitly discovering relationships between components and systems through elaborating with thinking maps ($ES = 0.60$), scientific discourse or discussion ($ES = 0.82$), reciprocal teaching (ES 0.54), or a problem-solving task ($ES = 0.68$) similar to the one in Mr. Smith's chemistry classroom.

In the remainder of this chapter, we will examine deep learning of science content knowledge, along with process skills, and consider the use

a.

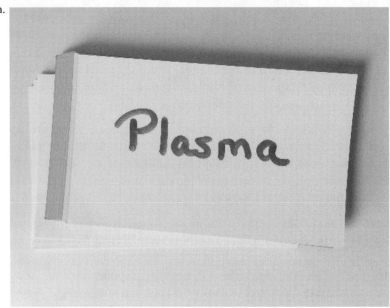

b.

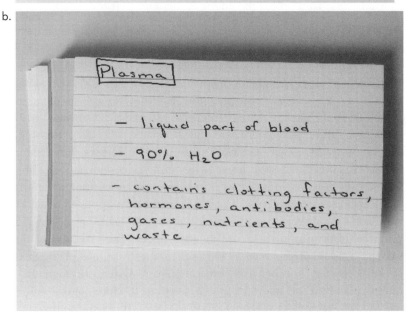

Figure 3.6

of high-impact approaches that foster recognizing relationships among the ideas acquired and consolidated during the surface learning phase. As in the previous chapter, we will first guide you in the selection of science learning tasks that promote deep learning, building on our examples of Mr. Smith and Ms. Easton. These include the following:

- Concept maps, or thinking maps
- Scientific discourse
- Reciprocal teaching
- Inquiry-based teaching

We will also discuss deep learning through the processes of science. These include

- Observing
- Classifying and sequencing
- Communicating
- Measuring
- Predicting
- Hypothesizing
- Inferring
- Using variables in experiments
- Designing, constructing, and interpreting models
- Interpreting, analyzing, and evaluating data

However, with regard to scientific processes, our attention will shift to those processes that support making connections and thinking meta-cognitively—that is, they prompt students to think about their thinking, discuss ideas, take action, and see errors. Specifically, we will look at designing, constructing, and interpreting models, as well as interpreting, analyzing, and evaluating data.

Selecting Science Tasks That Promote Deep Learning

Tasks that have the greatest impact on deep student learning are those that link and integrate content, providing a more coherent understanding of how individual terms, ideas, and concepts within science content knowledge can be synthesized into a broader scientific principle or phenomenon. Among other things, deep science learners are able to extract relationships from data and evidence to make and justify a claim. For example, a learner not only can identify that earthquakes are more frequent along tectonic plate boundaries and where these boundaries are located on Earth (surface learning); she can also justify why earthquakes are more frequent at these locations (deep learning). As another example, consider a learner who not only can engage in a laboratory investigation using a spring scale, a steel plate, and masses to determine the coefficient of kinetic friction; he or she can also identify the relevant data necessary to determine this value as well as critically evaluate the reasonableness of the calculation. This student can answer and justify his or her answer to questions such as the following: Should the coefficient of friction have been the same in all three trials? What conditions may have caused differences in your coefficient calculations?

As learners transition from surface learning to deep learning, the nature of their thinking transitions from quantitative to qualitative. During the surface learning phase, students are building more science content knowledge and process skills and thus increasing the number of terms, ideas, and concepts for which they have conceptual understanding. When learners progress into deeper learning, students extend their understanding of these existing terms, ideas, and concepts by forming relationships and generalizations. This is a qualitative change in their thinking. Instead of learning more, learners begin to learn how and why.

Video 3.2
Learning Intentions

*http://resources.corwin
.com/vl-science*

As with surface learning, the SOLO Taxonomy (Biggs & Collis, 1982) provides the framework for this progression, supporting the alignment of learning intentions, success criteria, and the selection of tasks. Deep learning is represented by the relational level of thinking. Referring back to earthquakes and the laboratory investigation of kinetic friction, Table 3.2 shows the progression of learning intentions and success criteria.

Notice the change in the level of the thinking as well as the nature of the thinking. In both of the examples, learners progress from knowing more about geoscience processes to knowing how and why they occur. In terms of the SOLO Taxonomy, learners are focusing not just on a single idea (uni-structural) or multiple ideas (multi-structural), but on the interaction between these ideas.

SOLO TAXONOMY LEVELS: PROGRESSION TO DEEP LEARNING (RELATIONAL LEVEL)

SOLO Level	Learning Intention	Success Criteria
Uni-structural	I understand that the Earth's surface is composed of tectonic plates.	I can identify plate boundaries.
Multi-structural	I understand that certain geoscience or Earth processes occur at tectonic plate boundaries.	I can describe Earth processes that occur at tectonic plate boundaries. I can explain that certain geoscience or Earth processes occur at tectonic plate boundaries.
Relational	I understand that the type of geoscience or Earth processes depends on the movement of tectonic plates.	I can explain how the movement of tectonic plates is related to specific geoscience or Earth processes.

SOLO Level	Learning Intention	Success Criteria
Uni-structural	I understand that friction opposes motion.	I can define friction.
Multi-structural	I understand that friction occurs with both moving and stationary objects.	I can describe static and kinetic friction. I can identify examples of static and kinetic friction.
Relational	I understand that the type of friction depends on the physical characteristics of the object.	I can explain how the frictional force on an object is related to the physical characteristics of the object.

Table 3.2

COMPARING DIFFICULTY
AND COMPLEXITY

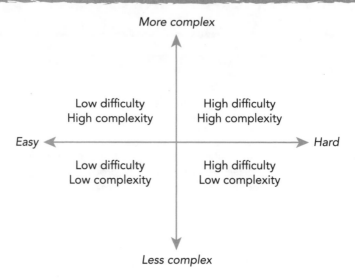

Figure 3.7

This progression to deep learning also provides additional opportunities to adjust the rigor of the learning experiences. Deep learning tasks should increase in both difficulty and complexity, although maybe not at the same time.

If you recall, surface learning is commonly associated with low difficulty and low complexity (see Figure 3.7). Deeper learning should move learning experiences or tasks toward a higher level of complexity and, in some cases, a higher level of difficulty. The series of question-based tasks in Mr. Smith's chemistry classroom provides an example of monitoring the level of difficulty, but maintaining a high level of complexity for all learners. There is a difference in the level of difficulty between each of the questions:

1. Is the boiling point of an element a periodic property?

2. Is the melting point of an element a periodic property?

3. Is atomic mass a periodic property?

4. Is atomic radius a periodic property?

5. Is ionic radius a periodic property?

6. Is the ionization energy of an atom a periodic property?

7. Is the electron affinity of an atom a periodic property?

Each question asks students to investigate the relationship between atomic properties and the arrangement of the periodic table. However, the questions are set at different levels of difficulty, so that Mr. Smith can differentiate which particular group gets a particular question. This is not advocating for ability grouping, as we know the effect size associated with ability grouping is 0.12. However, in mixed-ability groups or groups based on interest, adjusting the level of difficulty while maintaining the level of complexity will allow learners to experience the complexity of the thinking designed by this task, but at the same time, it will reduce the language barrier or mathematical barrier that may get in the way of students' developing a deep understanding of the essential relationship being examined: The arrangement of the periodic table is related to specific properties of the elements or atoms. This was Mr. Smith's learning intention.

Let's look at the examples of geoscience processes and friction. As learners strive to understand that the type of geoscience or Earth processes depends on the movement of tectonic plates, a teacher could reduce the level of difficulty by having learners focus on a specific region of the world with which they are familiar or limit the region of the globe on which they will focus. This reduces the amount of effort required to engage in the task without reducing the complexity of the thinking required to engage. A teacher could also reduce the amount of earthquake data available to learners, thus reducing the sheer amount of information available for analysis. On the other hand, a teacher could increase the difficulty by providing earthquake data (e.g., Richter scale readings, duration, epicenter location) and then have learners plot these data on a physical map. This increases the level of difficulty by requiring students to put more effort into the data analysis. Similarly, a teacher could reduce the difficulty in the coefficient of kinetic friction laboratory by scaffolding the mathematical aspect of the task with a spreadsheet formula or calculator and by providing a template for organizing the data collection aspect of the task. Difficulty could be increased by adding additional variables, such as calculating the coefficient of both a steel plate and a wooden block, as seen in Figure 3.8.

To increase the level of thinking, or complexity, for this task, learners might be required to use an inclined plane for the sliding surface, adding the additional relationship of height and angle of inclination.

INCREASING DIFFICULTY: COEFFICIENT CALCULATION EXAMPLE

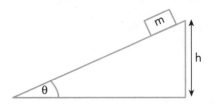

Figure 3.8

For earthquakes, learners might have to determine whether earthquake data are linked to the original earthquake or the result of aftershocks. In this case, the increase in complexity comes with the deeper understanding of the relationship between tectonic movement, earthquakes, and aftershocks. For deeper learning, added complexity should be the result of students' documenting evidence from multiple sources, supporting their claims, and explaining relationships between terms, ideas, and concepts. Keep in mind that as learners become successful at specific levels of complexity, they are ready to move to the next phase of their learning: transfer (which will be discussed in Chapter 4).

Deep Learning in Science Made Visible

To make deep learning visible in the science classroom, teachers must use the right strategy at the right time. We will explore the following high-impact instructional strategies for deep learning:

- Concept maps, or thinking maps
- Scientific discourse
- Reciprocal teaching
- Inquiry-based teaching

Concept Maps, or Thinking Maps

One way to help students identify relationships between terms, ideas, and concepts is to ask them to create a concept map, or thinking map

(*ES* = 0.64). Thinking maps are visual representations of knowledge that show relationships among concepts, processes, and other ideas though connecting lines and figures (Nesbit & Adesope, 2006). They don't work especially well at the surface level because students don't have the concepts needed to organize the relationships. David Ausubel (1968) found that learners actively subsume new concepts within a conceptual framework or structure of prior knowledge (Estes, Mills, & Barron, 1969). Through a concept map or thinking map, students are able to take new concepts and actively organize them into a visual representation that integrates their understanding of existing knowledge. When this type of map is used effectively, learners are able to visually represent relationships by actively and deliberately engaging with foundational knowledge acquired and consolidated during the surface learning phase. The visual representation makes students' deep learning visible to the teacher as well as to themselves.

Research on the instructional benefits of concept maps in instructional settings is quite positive. The use of concept maps is associated with an increase in encoding, retention, and recall (Nesbit & Adesope, 2006). From a meta-analysis of more than 500 peer-reviewed studies, researchers identified a variety of uses for concept maps, including individually and cooperatively generated maps from lectures or printed materials and maps used as advance organizers, collaboration tools, and standalone collections of information (Novak & Gowin, 1984; see also O'Donnell, Dansereau, & Hall, 2002). Studies indicate that when concept maps are used in conjunction with text or lectures, used to convert text into a visual representation, or used in cooperative learning tasks and peer teaching, students demonstrate a higher level of understanding and retention of knowledge (Griffin & Robinson, 2005; Horton et al., 1993).

How can concept maps or thinking maps be used in the classroom? The learners in Michael Graves's earth science class have just completed an activity in which each student group selected one layer of the atmosphere (troposphere, stratosphere, mesosphere, thermosphere, or exosphere) and created a visual summary of the layer. Each poster had to include a visual representation and essential knowledge related to that particular layer. This was a quick review activity from yesterday's class, which introduced the layers of the atmosphere. Mr. Graves now wants his learners to begin to see the relationship between each of the layers and the overall characteristics of the atmosphere.

Teacher: *As you return to your seats, please find a blank left page in your interactive notebooks.*

Mr. Graves pauses and waits for students to return to their seats and get their notebooks.

Teacher: *On that blank left page, draw a circle in the center of your paper that is about the size of an egg yolk. You will be using a variety of the colored markers at your table to arrange the words, phrases, or examples from your posters hanging on the wall into a mind map.*

Mr. Graves shows an example of a mind map.

Teacher: *Here is an example of a mind map. Notice how I have used colored lines to connect words, phrases, or examples together. Remember, you are encouraged to use pictures, words, phrases, or any other representation. Be creative and make it your own interpretation of the information. Take about 5 minutes to make your mind map. Please begin.*

Mr. Graves waits approximately 5 minutes for students to complete the task.

To further capitalize on students' prior knowledge, while at the same time deepening their understanding of that knowledge, Mr. Graves must take the mind mapping activity one step further. He then asks his students to select several words, phrases, or examples that they have linked together and write a complete sentence containing those words, phrases, or examples. For example, a student may have linked the terms *density* and *air pressure* with the layers. A sentence linking these words might be written as follows: "Layers of the atmosphere at higher altitudes are less dense and have less air pressure than layers of the atmosphere at lower altitudes." These assessment data make learning visible to both the students and Mr. Graves, and he can evaluate the data to make instructional decisions.

There are a variety of concept maps or thinking maps that provide a framework for linking and integrating content and offer a more coherent understanding of how individual terms, ideas, and concepts within science content knowledge can be synthesized into a broader scientific principle or phenomenon. Figures 3.9 through 3.13 present a few examples.

DOUBLE-BUBBLE MAP FOR COMPARING (E.G., COMPARING ANGIOSPERMS AND GYMNOSPERMS, VERTEBRATES AND INVERTEBRATES, COVALENT AND IONIC BONDS, COULOMB'S LAW AND UNIVERSAL LAW OF GRAVITATION)

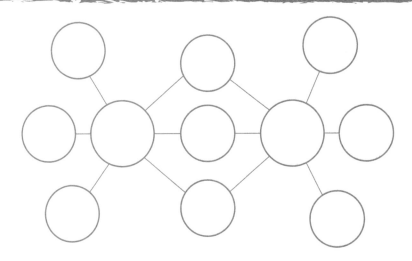

Figure 3.9

For thinking maps to be successful in deep learning, students must do more than fill in a map with information. Instead, the focus should be on the arrows or connectors in the map. These are the relationships between concepts.

Scientific Discourse

Within the scientific community, scientific discourse surrounds each and every discovery, theory, principle, or scientific law. As scientists engage in research, collect and analyze data, and make inferences, they must also construct and defend their scientific viewpoint. Through this discourse with their peers, scientists engage in the process of evaluating, modifying, and strengthening their understanding of the scientific phenomena in the universe. From cellular processes to constellations, our understanding of how the world works has grown out of

FLOW MAP FOR SEQUENCING (E.G., HISTORICAL DEVELOPMENT OF THE ATOM, CHEMICAL REACTIONS, GEOLOGIC TIME, CELLULAR PROCESSES)

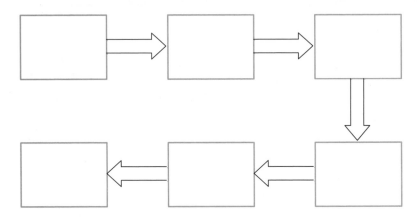

Figure 3.10

scientific discourse. Therefore, deep science learning should include a significant amount of classroom time devoted to student discourse and student-to-student interaction (i.e., classroom discussion, $ES = 0.82$). Scientific discourse should be qualitative, which is different from scientific explanations made during the surface phase of learning. During scientific explanations, learners are constructing meaning within specific content, engaging with those ideas through building consistent and coherent narratives. During scientific discourse, learners are negotiating understanding by making claims, supporting those claims with evidence, and striving to reach consensus about scientific ideas, theories, or principles. For example, there is a difference between learners discussing the conceptual idea of greenhouse gases (surface learning explanations) and using data and evidence to support or refute the claim that we are experiencing global warming as a result of human actions (deep learning discourse).

For deep science learning to be made visible through scientific discourse, collaborative and cooperative learning tasks must do the following:

MULTI-FLOW MAP FOR CAUSE AND EFFECT (E.G., NUCLEAR FUSION OR FISSION, HOMEOSTASIS, RESOURCE SCARCITY OR AVAILABILITY, SEVERE STORMS, EROSION)

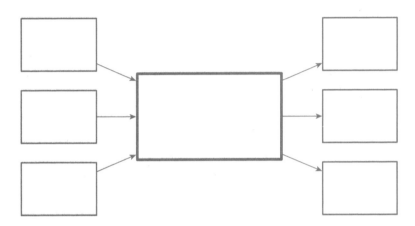

Figure 3.11

- Involve scientific ideas that are complex, so that learners must work together and will likely bring different strongly held viewpoints or perspectives to the task. Less complex tasks entice learners to divide and conquer the task or quickly "pick" one side or the other without any emotional investment. Also, the task should be complex enough for the number of students in the group. If there are too many students, someone might not participate.

- Allow for argumentation in which students agree and disagree with one another, negotiate understanding, make claims supported by reasons and evidence, and reach consensus or agree on where they disagree.

- Include sufficient language support, so that students know how to say what they want to say. This may mean cycling back through surface learning to teach vocabulary, provide sentence frames, or use teacher modeling.

BRACE MAP FOR PARTS AND WHOLE (E.G., PLANT CELLS, ATOMS AND MOLECULES, ECOSYSTEMS, GALAXIES, CLASSIFICATION SYSTEM, STANDARD UNITS OF MEASURE)

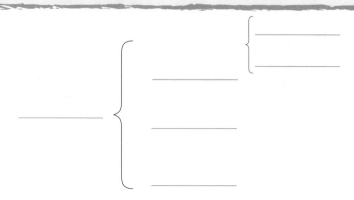

Figure 3.12

- Provide both individual and group accountability, so that learning is visible to students and teachers. In addition, these types of accountability prevent one student from completing the task for the other members of the group.

When these conditions are met, teachers allow learners to scaffold and support each other's thinking through discourse, rather than simply providing a venue for thinking aloud. However, this type of interaction requires structural support to ensure that learners focus on the task at hand and maintain a civil discourse. Learners can be supported during scientific discourse through role cards, contribution checklists, and individual accountability.

Role Cards

Role cards provide clear and structured tasks for each member of the collaborative team. Although the size of each discussion circle varies and ultimately is up to the teacher, forming groups of three to four students is most effective (Lou et al., 1996; Marzano, Pickering, & Pollock, 2001). Table 3.3 provides examples of discussion circle roles and tasks, which

TREE MAP FOR CLASSIFYING (E.G., SYSTEMS OF THE BODY, TYPES OF REACTIONS, BODIES OF WATER, COMPONENTS OF A CIRCUIT, FORCES, MATTER)

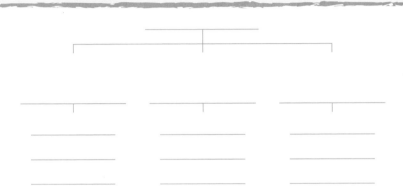

Figure 3.13

include discussion directors, or leaders; big idea builders, or summarizers; word wizards; map makers; and highlighters (Howard, 2010; Johnson & Johnson, 1999; Wilfong, 2012). Which roles are used in a specific discussion circle depends on the nature of the science content and the level of discourse necessary to uncover relationships between concepts.

Once students are preassigned to groups and their individual roles are determined, the teacher should provide ample time for the completion of individual tasks.

One approach to grouping students for collaborative tasks is alternate ranking (Fisher, Everlove, & Frey, 2009). Alternate ranking is based on assessment data and the specific learning needs of students for specific content. Again, this approach to flexible grouping requires teachers to have evidence of their students' thinking and learning.

Using assessment data, a teacher would first rank students based on their performances on a specific assessment. Starting at the top of the ranked list, the teacher would use student responses on the assessment to answer this question: Is this student making progress in his or her learning with

EXAMPLES OF DISCUSSION CIRCLE ROLES AND TASKS

Role	Task
Discussion director, or leader	Direct, lead, or guide the collaborative discourse. Monitor the classroom rules for discourse.
	Develop a set of critical thinking questions (not yes/no or one-word response questions) that encourage group members to make connections between the content, current events, other class topics, and/or group members' lives.
Big idea builder, or summarizer	Develop a list of the big ideas addressed during the discourse.
	Create a visual or written summary of the content.
	Be responsible for helping summarize the perspectives and viewpoints of each group member.
Word wizard	Identify key vocabulary terms or concepts.
	Prepare a description of each vocabulary term or concept.
	Create a visual for each item.
	Identify a specific example of each item.
	Provide locations or further information about each vocabulary term or concept.
Map maker	Create a concept map of the material.
	Develop an explanation of why certain concepts are connected together on the concept map.
Highlighter	Identify important readings, sections, or passages that are important.
	Mark these passages with a sticky note or tab.
	Provide a justification of why particular readings, sections, or passages were selected.

Table 3.3

the planned instruction? If yes, then the teacher would move down to the next student. When the teacher arrives at a student for whom the planned instruction is not supporting progress toward the learning intention and success criteria, the teacher would draw a line *above* this student's name. Now, moving to the bottom of the ranked list, the teacher would use student responses on the assessment to answer this question: Does this student need extensive support to make progress in his or her learning? If the answer is yes, the teacher would move up to the next student. When the teacher arrives at a student who does not need extensive support, but is not making the expected learning gains with the planned instruction, the teacher would draw a line *below* this student's name (Fisher et al., 2009). This process provides three different groups, with different instructional needs, for a specific set of content.

As a word of caution, this process should not result in students' being placed in these groups for the remainder of the unit, semester, or year. This would be ability grouping, and this form of ability-level grouping ($ES = 0.12$) should be used rarely or sparingly, as it produces mixed results based on ability level. Alternate ranking is a flexible grouping strategy that is supported by assessment data and based on students' instructional needs for specific content ($ES = 1.07$ for response to intervention, or RTI). Learners are then grouped for collaborative learning based on that specific need and not a general label or ability ($ES = 0.61$ for not labeling students). A student who needs no additional support in understanding cellular processes may find that he or she needs scaffolding in understanding abiotic and biotic factors in terrestrial or aquatic ecosystems. Another example is when a student has a strong understanding of series and parallel circuits but requires extensive support in understanding energy transformation. In each of these examples, the student's group would change and thus is flexible.

Contribution Checklists

A teacher can provide a checklist of ways in which students can contribute to scientific discourse. These lists can include student behaviors such as asking questions, checking others' work, keeping the team on task, encouraging others respectfully, making sure the answer makes sense, making sure everyone can explain the reasoning, and drawing connections to things they've already learned. These lists can also include more task-specific roles, such as "checking the units." The behaviors can be listed on a poster, projected onto a screen, taped to students' tables, or

SAMPLE CHECKLIST

Have you considered . . .

- ☐ Asking questions of others to support their thinking?
- ☐ Checking your own and others' work for accuracy?
- ☐ Keeping the team on task?
- ☐ Encouraging others respectfully by providing positive comments?
- ☐ Making sure the answer makes sense and, if not, figuring out why?
- ☐ Making sure everyone can explain the reasoning for the answer?
- ☐ Drawing connections between this problem and other types of problems or tasks?
- ☐ Sketching a visual representation of the task you're trying to solve?
- ☐ Looking for another way to solve the task?
- ☐ Suggesting tools that might help your teammates approach the task?
- ☐ Drawing connections between the task and your real-world experience?

Figure 3.14

inserted into table tents, which are inexpensive pieces of plastic that hold paper in a vertical position on a table so that it is in students' line of sight. A sample checklist is included in Figure 3.14.

Teachers must provide support for learners as they develop the skills necessary for holding their peers accountable for their ideas, viewpoints, and perspectives. Providing accountability prompts, and modeling them, communicates volumes about the expectations for classroom discourse. Examples of these teacher prompts (Michaels, O'Connor, Hall, & Resnick, 2010) include the following:

- *Marking the conversation:* "That's an important point."
- *Challenging students:* "What do you think about that question Samuel asked?"
- *Keeping everyone together:* "Who can repeat what Rachael just said, using your own words?"

EXAMPLES OF PROMPTS

Prompt	Examples
Press for clarification and explanation	• Could you describe what you mean? • Can you provide an example that supports your claim? • Can you tell me more about your thinking about . . . ?
Require justification of proposals and challenges	• Where did you find that information? • How did you know that? • How does that support your claim?
Recognize and challenge misconceptions	• I don't agree because . . . • Have you considered an alternative such as . . . ? • I think that there is a misconception here, specifically . . .
Require evidence for claims and arguments	• Can you give me an example? • Where did you find that information? • How does this evidence support your claim?
Interpret and use each other's statements	• David suggested . . . • What I heard Marla say was . . . • I was thinking about Jackson's idea, and I think . . .

Table 3.4

- *Keeping the channels open:* "Did everyone hear that? Jessica, can you say that again?"

- *Linking contributions:* "Kelsey, can you put your idea together with the one Oliver just suggested?"

- *Pressing for accuracy:* "Where can we find that?"

- *Pressing for reasoning:* "Why do you think so?"

- *Building on prior knowledge:* "Tara, how does your idea connect with what we've been studying?"

- *Verifying and clarifying:* "I want to make sure I understand. Are you saying . . . ?"

As with the contribution checklist, making these prompts visible to both the teacher and the learners provides cues for engaging in effective and civil discourse (see Table 3.4).

Individual Accountability

When individual accountability is warranted, the first (and possibly easiest) layer of accountability you can offer students is to add a deliverable or product that must be completed during the scientific discourse. For example, learners might have to complete a concept map or thinking map. Learners may be asked to provide a written analysis of the discourse. While having everyone in a group record the group's thinking with this deliverable or product won't guarantee that they all learn, it does increase the likelihood of positive outcomes. Round robin writing is a technique where each student is provided with a different colored marker. Learners must then contribute to a poster by recording their thoughts or responses to questions about the discourse. The previous question stems provide a starting point for this strategy. At a glance, you can see who contributed ideas, to what extent, and whether they need more guidance. Students are likely to be thinking about what they're writing and to critique or accept one another's reasoning as they're writing it down and are less likely to tune out if they have to produce something.

Some learners may need time to formulate their thoughts or consider ideas individually before engaging with peers. In these cases, the teacher can structure students' thinking time so that they can answer four questions for themselves prior to engaging with the group:

1. What is the question asking?
2. What useful information is given?
3. What other information would be helpful?
4. What might an answer look like?

Whether or not students are able to answer all four questions, the time spent reflecting on these questions increases the likelihood that they'll be able to contribute to the collaboration. Students may respond to the questions in writing or by creating models, charts, diagrams, concept maps, or thinking maps. This access to multiple representations gives more ready access to each learner and encourages later conversation about how various representations relate to one another. This individual exploration time sets the stage for individual accountability by ensuring that each group member has ideas to share.

Individual accountability can also be accomplished in task design. In their fourth-grade classroom, the students in Heather Birko's class were studying biomes and ecosystems. The groups had several tasks to complete. The first was to write a report on their assigned biome and develop a presentation for their peers that would be recorded as a screen cast. The groups were expected to collaborate on the report and the presentation, and they were given role sheets to do so. In addition, each student had to select an animal or plant that lived in the biome to investigate further. The checklist included information that was required for the specific animal or plant, including reasons why it survived in the biome, whether there were other biomes where it could survive, and data about the population as well as predictions for the future of that plant or animal.

Reciprocal Teaching

What each of the previously described high-impact instructional strategies has in common is student ownership of learning. Whether through the development of concept maps or thinking maps or preparing for and engaging in scientific discourse, learners in each of the previous scenarios are expected to take ownership of their learning by actively and deliberately engaging in the discovery and understanding of scientific content. Furthermore, learners are then held accountable by their peers as they participate in scientific discourse. In the end, this provides multiple opportunities for learners to assume the role of teacher and teach their peers. Reciprocal teaching, or allowing students to teach each other,

SAMPLE GRAPH USED TO SHOW STUDENTS SEASONAL PATTERNS

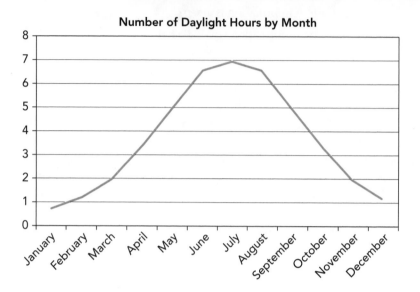

Figure 3.15

has a large impact on student learning (*ES* = 0.74). These strategies create a classroom environment that encourages learners to ask questions about the content and use process skills to seek answers to those questions.

This is exactly what Mrs. Leonard does with her first graders. During the year, Mrs. Leonard has devoted significant learning time for her students to make predictions, summarize their learning, clarify understanding, and generate questions. Although the science block is one timespan for this learning, Mrs. Leonard has also helped learners develop these skills through their mathematics and literacy blocks. Today she is going to use reciprocal teaching to deepen her learners' understanding of how these processes can be used to understand seasonal patterns by analyzing and interpreting data related to sunrise, sunset, and seasonal patterns.

Learners are placed into collaborative learning groups using the previously described alternate ranking process. Mrs. Leonard shares with the students that they will be making predictions, summarizing their ideas, clarifying their explanations, and developing questions about scientific data. She models this process by presenting data on a graph (see Figure 3.15).

Mrs. Leonard models the teaching of each of the processes. She summarizes the data presented in the graph, makes predictions about the location in which these data were collected, clarifies the patterns observed in the data, and develops a series of questions about the data. Mrs. Leonard then provides each student with a graph generated from different sets of data, from different locations in the world. Each student then takes a turn teaching the processes to the group using his or her assigned data.

There are four processes that students have to understand at the surface level for reciprocal teaching to work: predicting, summarizing, clarifying, and questioning. If students do not understand these cognitive processes, this instructional routine will not likely work. When it does work, students have a powerful interaction with their peers and texts, in which they uncover a lot of information and make connections with what they already know (Rosenshine & Meister, 1994).

Inquiry-Based Teaching

Inquiry-based teaching has an overall effect size of 0.40. This, of course, is less than 1 year's worth of growth. This relatively small effect size is due, in part, to the timing of this approach. Inquiry-based teaching is less effective when used at the surface phase of learning. However, when used during the deep phase of the learning process, inquiry-based teaching provides an environment for learners to actively and deliberately engage in the discovery and understanding of scientific content. Timing matters.

Inquiry-based teaching involves (1) the hook, (2) the formulation of questions, (3) selecting a question, (4) peer collaboration, (5) answering the question, (6) sharing findings, and (7) evaluation and assessment. Expert teachers know their students, and they use data from pre-assessments to adapt or optimize their instruction with timely interventions during the learning process when learners need to cycle back to surface learning.

Mr. Knod has launched his fifth graders into a learning experience, confident that he has spent time activating his students' prior knowledge and developing their background knowledge where necessary. They are ready to make observations and measurements and to use those data to classify minerals (NGSS Lead States, 2013). Students must know key vocabulary and enter with some basic knowledge about the physical properties of minerals (NGSS Lead States, 2013). Mr. Knod is well aware that during this activity, vocabulary may need to be revisited and clarified. To start, the students are put into groups of four. Mr. Knod asks the person who woke up the latest this morning to come get the necessary supplies. Within the bag are the following items: a glass plate, various types of minerals, a streak plate, and a magnifying glass. With little input from the teacher, each team is directed to examine and discuss everything they know about the materials provided in their supply baskets.

Upon completion of the discussion, Mr. Knod walks around the room, giving each group a bag. As he distributes these bags, he offers the entire group this scenario: "Due to your vast knowledge of rocks and minerals, you are now employed by our local museum. As you return to work after your lunch break, the head custodian hands you a mineral and tells you he found it on the floor. That mineral is in the bag I just gave you. It does not have a label. Your team must explain what process you would go through to correctly identify that mineral. Use what you already know about the properties of minerals."

Before the students get started, Mr. Knod continues to communicate the learning intention and success criteria. He reminds his learners to use their contribution checklists and question prompts to ensure collaborative group work to perform the investigation, and he reinforces the expectation that students will use physical properties to identify the mineral and that their explanations will include the key vocabulary that was addressed during the direct instruction portion of this unit.

The importance of ensuring that learning is visible to the teacher and the students can never be overstated. Inquiry-based teaching is an intentional and purposeful decision that learners are ready to explore the content with an increased level of independence. Learning needs to be fostered and supported, but not in the same structured fashion of direct instruction. As teachers frontload the experience with relevant "hooks," stimulate curiosity with authentic engaging scenarios, and check students' level of understanding, they become confident that with the use of essential questions, students will explore the learning.

Scientific Processes and Thinking

As learners work to uncover the relationships between terms, concepts, and ideas within that topic, they also develop a deeper understanding of the process skills necessary to reveal those relationships. For example, learners no longer identify properties of an object from a single

SOLO TAXONOMY LEVELS: SURFACE AND DEEP LEARNING OF SCIENTIFIC PROCESSES AND THINKING

SOLO Level	Learning Intention	Success Criteria
Uni-structural	I understand that the characteristics of objects are identified by direct observation.	I can identify the properties of an object by using my senses.
Multi-structural	I understand that observations can be made from multiple perspectives.	I can describe an object from different positions. I can identify differences in an object from different perspectives.
Relational	I understand that observations provide data for developing scientific questions.	I can relate my predictions and scientific questions to specific observations. I can describe the relationship between observing and formulating questions.

Table 3.5

perspective or multiple perspectives. To understand relationships in science content, the process skills must support that understanding. Learners must make observations and then use those observations to formulate questions. This deep understanding of what it means to observe requires that learners understand the relationship between observations and their own personal interpretations of those observations. Table 3.5 adds to the SOLO progression from the previous chapter, taking the progression from surface learning to deep learning.

Deep learning of science content knowledge goes hand in hand with deeper learning of process skills in science. There is a deep learning phase for the scientific processes of observing; classifying and sequencing;

communicating; measuring; predicting; hypothesizing; inferring; using variables in experiments; designing, constructing, and interpreting models; and interpreting, analyzing, and evaluating data. Let's look more closely at two specific process skills associated with deep learning: (1) interpreting, analyzing, and evaluating data and (2) designing, constructing, and interpreting models:

PROCESS PROGRESSION CHART FOR INTERPRETING, ANALYZING, AND EVALUATING DATA

1. Unusual or unexpected results in an activity are recognized.

2. Observations and data are recorded, analyzed, and communicated orally and with simple graphs, pictures, written statements, and numbers.

3. Data are analyzed, and unexpected or unusual quantitative data are recognized.

4. Unexpected or unusual quantitative data are recognized.

5. Numerical data that are contradictory or unusual in experimental results are recognized.

6. Data are collected, recorded, analyzed, and communicated using proper graphical representations and metric measurements.

7. Patterns are identified in data and are interpreted and evaluated.

8. Data tables showing the independent and dependent variables, derived quantities, and the number of trials are constructed and interpreted. Data tables for descriptive statistics showing specific measures of central tendency, the range of the data set, and the number of repeated trials are constructed and interpreted.

9. Valid conclusions are made after analyzing data.

10. Scales, diagrams, charts, graphs, tables, imagery, models, and profiles are constructed and interpreted.

11. Conclusions are formed based on recorded quantitative and qualitative data.

12. Alternative scientific explanations and models are recognized and analyzed.

13. Mathematical manipulations are explored, including SI units, scientific notation, linear equations, graphing, ratio and proportion, significant digits, and dimensional analysis.

14. Models and simulations are used to visualize and explain phenomena, to make predictions from hypotheses, and to interpret data. (adapted from VDOE, 2012)

As learners progress from focusing on single data points and whether they do or do not make sense (uni-structural level), they begin to develop ways to organize and communicate multiple data points. When learners have developed proficiency in these foundational process skills (i.e., collecting, organizing, and displaying multiple data points), they are ready to look for relationships in the data. This requires students to select which representation of the data is most appropriate for recognizing these relationships or patterns. A learning progression for this particular process skill might look like the one in Table 3.6.

A similar approach can be taken with modeling. As learners seek to develop deep understanding of scientific phenomena, they will likely encounter a situation where the "real thing" is not realistically possible (e.g., nuclear fusion, atomic structure, catalysts, astronomical units). Therefore, learners must develop physical or mathematical representations of phenomena that serve the purpose of this deeper understanding (Gilbert, 2004; Gilbert, Boulter, & Elmer, 2000). Models can be used to (1) develop more concrete or simple representations of ideas or concepts, (2) give learners a chance to visualize scientific principles that cannot be realistically observed in the classroom, and (3) provide an anchor for explaining and discussing ideas (Coll & Lajium, 2011).

SOLO TAXONOMY LEVELS: SKILLS FOR IDENTIFYING DATA RELATIONSHIPS

SOLO Level	Learning Intention	Success Criteria
Uni-structural	I understand that observations provide me with data.	I can record data from an observation.
Multi-structural	I understand that data can be organized and communicated in multiple ways.	I can represent data graphically, with pictures, through written statements, and with numbers.
Relational	I understand that data can be analyzed to find patterns.	I can explain the relationship between types of data and how to best represent the data. I can use my representations of data to describe patterns.

Table 3.6

A learning progression for this particular process skill might look like the one in Table 3.7.

As we have discussed before, learners must engage in scientific thinking that builds on their foundational knowledge about how we do science. Scientific process skills develop or progress through purposefully and intentionally designed learning experiences. Before learners dive deeply into scientific processes, they must have the foundational knowledge to do so.

Feedback

Returning to the feedback chart from the previous chapter (repeated here as Figure 3.16), effective feedback is defined as information that closes the gap between where learners are and where they are headed (i.e., learning intention and success criteria). Effective feedback is information

PROCESS PROGRESSION CHART FOR DESIGNING, CONSTRUCTING, AND INTERPRETING MODELS

1. Simple physical models are designed and constructed to clarify explanations and show relationships.

2. Models are constructed to clarify explanations, demonstrate relationships, and solve needs.

3. Scale models are used to estimate distance, volume, and quantity.

4. Models and simulations are designed and used to illustrate and explain phenomena and systems.

5. Models and simulations are constructed and used to illustrate and explain phenomena.

6. Technologies, including computers, probe ware, and geospatial technologies, are used to collect, analyze, and report data and to demonstrate concepts and simulate experimental conditions.

7. Maps and globes are read and interpreted, including location by latitude and longitude.

8. Alternative scientific explanations and models are recognized and analyzed.

9. Models and simulations are used to visualize and explain phenomena, to make predictions from hypotheses, and to interpret data. (adapted from VDOE, 2012)

about learning that reminds learners of what they are learning, how they are progressing in that learning, and where they are going next with their learning.

For the deep stage of the learning process, process feedback is very important as learners explore the why and the how of science content knowledge and process skills. At this point in the learning process,

SOLO TAXONOMY LEVELS: DESIGNING, CONSTRUCTING, AND INTERPRETING MODELS

SOLO Level	Learning Intention	Success Criteria
Uni-structural	I understand that physical models help me represent a concept.	I can identify a model of a scientific phenomenon.
Multi-structural	I understand that models help me explain complex ideas.	I can use a model to explain my thinking.
Relational	I understand that models support my problem solving.	I can select a model that best supports my problem solving. I can develop a model that helps me solve a problem.

Table 3.7

students have identified clear boundaries between concepts and are aware of examples and non-examples associated with a specific concept. In their surface learning, students assimilated task feedback into their work to develop a conceptual understanding of boiling point, melting point, ionization energy, and electron affinity. This is the same for earthquakes and friction. However, to move learners beyond what is simply right or wrong or an example or non-example, they must receive and incorporate feedback that focuses on the process or strategies associated with accomplishing a specific task.

Process feedback supports self-explanation, self-monitoring, self-questioning, and critical thinking. For example, a teacher may not tell a learner that his or her calculation of the coefficient of friction is wrong. Instead, the teacher may ask the learner what strategies he or she used in making the calculation. Rather than focusing on the correct answer regarding the relationship between tectonic plate movement and earthquakes, a teacher may ask a student, "What is your explanation for your answer?"

EFFECTIVE FEEDBACK CHART

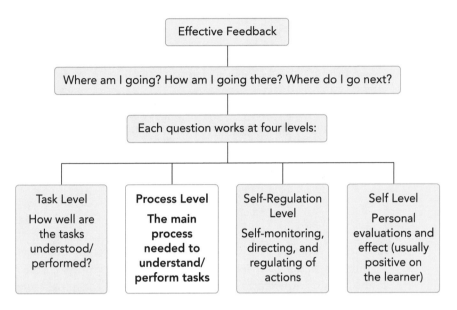

Effective Feedback

Where am I going? How am I going there? Where do I go next?

Each question works at four levels:

Task Level	Process Level	Self-Regulation Level	Self Level
How well are the tasks understood/performed?	**The main process needed to understand/perform tasks**	Self-monitoring, directing, and regulating of actions	Personal evaluations and effect (usually positive on the learner)

Source: Based on Hattie and Timperley (2007).

Figure 3.16

The focus of process feedback is on relationships between ideas, students' strategies for evaluating the reasonableness of an answer or solution, explicitly learning from mistakes, and helping the learner identify different strategies for addressing a task.

Process feedback should be specific and constructive and should support learners' pathways toward self-regulation feedback. Put another way, learners know what to do, when they don't know what to do, and the teacher is not available. Effective feedback is characterized by not only the type of feedback (i.e., task, process, and self-regulation) but also the specificity and constructive nature of the feedback. Does the teacher prompt learners through strategic questioning related to the learning process? What appears to be wrong, and why? What approach or strategies did the student use? What is an explanation for the answer, response, or solution? What other questions can the teacher ask about the task? What are the relationships with other parts of the task? These

Video 3.3
Effective Feedback

*http://resources.corwin
.com/vl-science*

prompts offer opportunities for learners to engage in self-explanation ($ES = 0.50$), self-monitoring ($ES = 0.45$), and self-verbalizing the steps in a problem ($ES = 0.41$). These effect sizes are associated with the consolidation of deep learning (Hattie & Donoghue, 2016).

To successfully assimilate process feedback and use it to make decisions about where to go next in their learning, students must have the foundational knowledge to understand both what the feedback means and possible options for making adjustments and moving forward. Effective feedback and effective use of that feedback support the acquisition and consolidation of deep learning and move the learner closer to self-regulation.

Conclusion

As teachers recognize that the learners in their classrooms are progressing in their thinking and learning, they must make precise adjustments to the learning experiences to scaffold this progress. The initial acquisition and consolidation of terms, ideas, or concepts in science represents a quantitative increase in content knowledge and process skills. When teachers and students are mindful of successful surface learning, they can leverage what students know by deepening this knowledge and focusing on qualitative aspects of learning: the why and the how. The necessary foundational knowledge associated with a particular segment of science content knowledge, along with the process skills needed to actively engage with the content, must be used in learning experiences or tasks that elaborate on this initial learning, must actively and deliberately engage learners with data and evidence so that they can discover and understand the underlying scientific principle, and must move away from treating each idea as an independent scientific phenomenon. When science learning is visible to both the teacher and his or her learners, this visibility takes students one step closer to applying their learning to new contexts or problems: This is transfer, which will be discussed in the next chapter.

Reflection Questions

1. Consider the science topics for your grade level. What is the deep learning phase of each topic? What would that look like in the relational level of a SOLO chart? What specific strategies might you use to help students actively and deliberately engage with data and evidence to understand the underlying scientific principle?

2. How do you determine when your learners are progressing to deeper learning? What evidence do you collect? Do you share this evidence with your learners? Why or why not?

3. How often do learners have the opportunity to make their thinking visible? What opportunities do students have to represent their thinking using concept maps or thinking maps? What strategies could you use to provide additional opportunities for students to show relationships between science terms, ideas, or concepts?

4. What is the role of questioning in your classroom? How do you model self-questioning, self-verbalization, and critical thinking in science? Are students encouraged to engage in questioning and discourse with their peers? What strategies can you use to encourage students to use questioning as a form of feedback for their peers? What tools could you make available to your students to help support their questioning and feedback with peers?

SCIENCE TRANSFER LEARNING MADE VISIBLE

4

The transfer of learning to different contexts or problems, both inside and outside the classroom, is the ultimate goal in science teaching and learning. The ability for a learner to utilize science content knowledge and process skills in one setting and then again in a different setting paves the way for innovation. Transfer requires that learners assimilate the right combination of science knowledge and process skills that apply to the different context or problem. Successfully bringing together the right mix of learning allows students to solve problems such as space junk, the Pacific Ocean garbage patch, climate change, endangered species, and water scarcity. To be successful, they must (1) have the strong foundation of a conceptual understanding of the necessary content, (2) understand complex relationships between a multitude of science content, and (3) test and discern possible combinations that work in the different setting.

Consider the act of tying your shoes. Although this process took considerable effort, time, and deliberate practice when you were younger and first learning the skill and process, most readers of this book are now able to tie the laces of any type of footwear. From sneakers to snow boots, when we put on a different pair of shoes, tie the shoelaces of a young child, or assist anyone with the tying of their shoes, we easily accomplish this task. Why? Transfer. Most of us have a strong foundation of the conceptual understanding of shoes, shoelaces, and the process of tying. We have "overlearned" how to tie laces; we no longer have to expend working memory on this task—it has become automatic. We also understand the relationship between types of shoes, laces, and the specific components involved in lacing them up. And, finally, we have considerable experience testing and discerning possible combinations that work in this different setting (sneakers, snow boots, shoes with Velcro, etc.). This specific example likely has helped you conceptualize the idea of learning transfer because you have engaged in a bit of transfer as you have read this particular section of the book. This example has provided a close association between a previously learned task (i.e., shoe tying) and a different context or problem (i.e., the teaching and learning of science). This is necessary for promoting transfer.

There are several reasons why the shoe example works, and they have everything to do with methods for promoting transfer of learning. The first reason this example works is because it is a situation nearly every adult—and certainly every parent—has experienced, and it is therefore immediately relatable. Even if you do not have children of your own, as a teacher, you likely have tied the shoes of a young child. Furthermore, you have probably worn a tie or neck scarf to parent-teacher conferences. Same idea! As we mentioned earlier, close association between a previously learned task and a new situation is necessary for promoting transfer of learning. A second reason this works is because there is an analogy at play here, in this case comparing the tying of shoes to complex learning. But this falls apart if we use this example with someone who has never owned a pair of shoes or a pair of shoes with laces. A limiting factor in fostering transfer is in pairing the experience with the knowledge base of the learner. With no knowledge base for shoes or shoelaces, we would need to find a different example. That brings us to the third reason: Knowing the learner developmentally and experientially is essential when promoting transfer of learning.

But there's one more factor, and perhaps the most critical one: We have the cognitive and metacognitive skills to detect the similarities and differences from one situation to another. In our shoe tying analogy, we know up front that the key differences are the type of shoe, the type of laces, the specific length of the laces, and whether or not the shoe actually has laces. Having the skills to detect similarities and differences is key to transfer—without this, we may transfer the wrong ideas from our previous pair of shoes. Thus, a pair of slip-ons or shoes without laces would leave us paralyzed with confusion.

Throughout the previous chapters, we have devoted significant time to examples of surface and deep learning in science classrooms. We will revisit a few of these examples and see how learners would transfer their learning within these classrooms. With the transfer of learning, there are a few key points to consider:

1. Surface learning and deep learning are necessary for transfer. When learners do not have a strong conceptual understanding or the foundational knowledge of a specific topic, transfer is not likely to happen.

2. Shallow, or highly contextualized, learning will reduce the likelihood of transfer. In other words, without actively uncovering relationships among science concepts, transfer is not likely to happen.

3. Transfer is an active process that comes from the purposeful and intentional selection of tasks that provide learners with explicit opportunities to transfer their learning to a new context.

In science, transfer learning is the movement from learning about scientific laws, principles, theories, and phenomena to learning to use these ideas to solve problems within different contexts. Many of these contexts are multidisciplinary. For example, biology students may learn about cellular processes—in particular, diffusion, osmosis, and movement of molecules (e.g., ions and proteins) across the cellular membrane. This foundational knowledge is crucial in developing new technologies for kidney dialysis. The innovation of kidney dialysis transferred foundational knowledge, processes, and complex relationships between ideas such as the movement of materials across a membrane, cellular processes, and the physiological processes of the human body to the lifesaving technology of dialysis. This transfer was possible because of strong surface learning, deep learning, and the cognitive and metacognitive skills needed to detect the similarities and differences between these ideas and kidney failure.

From the perspective of other disciplines, learners acquire mathematics knowledge and procedural fluency in mathematical functions. This learning is necessary for successful modeling in science. In a fifth-grade classroom, learners were asked to create mass-versus-volume plots for three different substances. To generate the data for such a plot, collaborative learning groups had to manipulate the independent variable by varying the volume of each substance and then finding the associated mass. When these data were plotted on the same graph for each of the three substances (see Figure 4.1), learners were asked to interpret the plot and determine the density of each substance.

To successfully create the mass-versus-volume plot, analyze the mathematical model, and interpret the relationship between mass and volume, students had to transfer their learning from linear functions and slope to the calculation of the density for a specific substance.

Transfer Learning

In the science classroom, the ultimate goal is transfer. As science teachers, we want our learners to transfer their surface and deep knowledge and understanding to new situations. We do not have false expectations that each learner in our classroom will become a scientist. Thus, this transfer can manifest itself as pursuing a research career in science, serving as a practitioner in a health or medical field, or being a scientifically literate and informed citizen who applies science learning to his or her daily life (when recycling, voting, etc.). Author John (Hattie, 2009)

MASS-VERSUS-VOLUME
PLOTS FOR THREE SUBSTANCES

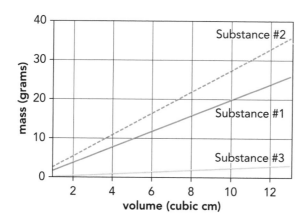

Figure 4.1

explains that transfer learning is about the ways in which students construct knowledge and reality for themselves as a consequence of surface and deep knowing and understanding. As learners progress through the learning process, the route is not clear-cut and often involves a nonlinear pathway. As mentioned earlier, learners may have to go back to pick up necessary surface learning about particular science content. In addition, transfer learning can happen quickly and spark the need for new surface learning. For example, a student may transfer his or her learning to a new situation but then ask a new question that requires the need for new surface learning. Consider Ms. Cross's classroom from Chapter 2. A seventh grader in her classroom may quickly transfer the learning from the panther activity to the local debate about the construction of a gas pipeline and its potential impact on the local wildlife. However, this transfer may also spawn questions about which energy source is most cost-effective and environmentally safe. This will likely prompt the need for new surface learning about renewable and nonrenewable resources and the economics of energy consumption.

One concern is that science instruction too often stops at the surface level of learning, and students (particularly struggling students) either fail to go deep and transfer or transfer *without* detecting similarities and differences between phenomena. When this happens, the transfer does not make sense, and too often students see this as evidence that they can't do science. For example, we may focus too much time on labeling the parts of a flower, identifying the different types of clouds, applying an algorithm to solving equations in physics, or memorizing the periodic table of elements. The task of teaching and learning best comes together when we attend to all three levels: ideas, thinking, and constructing.

Transfer is both a goal of learning and also a mechanism for propelling learning to the next level. Transfer as a goal means that teachers want students to begin to take the reins of their own learning, engage in meta-cognitive thinking, and apply what they know to a variety of real-world contexts. It also prepares them to move through the progression of science learning as ideas build on each other across grade levels. Transfer happens when students reach into their toolbox and decide what tools to employ to solve new and complex problems on their own. When students reach this phase, learning has been accomplished.

Mr. Ross is a second-grade teacher. Over the past week, his learners have devoted significant time to setting up series and parallel circuits and evaluating the properties of each component of electrical circuits. In the end, Mr. Ross wants his learners to be able to evaluate which materials have the properties best suited for use in an electrical circuit (i.e., resistors, conductors, and insulators). To set up the learning environment for transfer learning, Mr. Ross makes his students private investigators for the day. He provides a scenario where several electronic devices, or electrical circuits, have been disassembled and their parts mixed up. The learners, working in investigative teams, are to decide which parts go with which electrical device. As part of the task, each team must develop an argument supporting their reconstruction of the electronic device. In this classroom, students must reach into their toolbox and decide which content knowledge and process skills will help them complete this task. Furthermore, students are taking the reins of their learning as they decide on the best strategies and approaches for developing the argument to go with this task. In addition, this task helps learners know the how and the why, along with being able to apply their own electrical circuits and the process skills of analyzing data, interpreting data, and constructing explanations. This, in turn, supports the learners' ability to answer these questions: What are we learning? Why are we learning it? How do we know we have learned it?

In science, transfer learning happens when students can make connections among scientific laws, principles, theories, and phenomena and then use those understandings to solve problems in unfamiliar situations, while at the same time being intentionally aware of what they are doing. This often comes in the form of students' asking themselves clarifying questions; they can do this because in the deep learning phase, they had teachers who modeled how to ask those questions. This is one of the essential characteristics of a visible science learner.

Visible science learners, or assessment-capable learners (*ES* = 1.44), are students who

1. Are active in their science learning. They deliberately and intentionally engage in science learning through asking themselves questions, monitoring their own learning, and taking the reins of their learning. The learning task in Mr. Ross's second-grade classroom provides the type of environment necessary for this to occur.

2. Can plan the next steps in their science learning. Because assessment-capable science learners take an active role, these students can plan their next steps and where they need to go next in their learning. Returning to Mr. Ross's classroom, his second graders are likely to know what additional tools they need to successfully move forward in the task.

3. Understand the assessment and feedback provided by their peers and their teacher. Assessment-capable science learners have a firm understanding of the information behind each assessment and the feedback exchanged in the classroom. Put differently, these learners know what each piece of feedback means with regard to making adjustments and continuing on in their learning.

Creating a classroom environment that focuses on transfer as the goal of learning provides the best environment for developing assessment-capable science learners.

As an example, students studying the mass-versus-volume plots in the earlier example must deliberately think about what information to collect, how to use the information in the data chart, and what mathematical tools to use (equations? tables? graphs?) to identify the type of relationship (linear? exponential?) between the variables of mass and volume. Students planting the school garden have to apply their knowledge of volume and some standard measures to determine how much mulch to buy to cover the garden plot. Using examples that relate authentic situations not only provides students with opportunities to develop transfer learning; it also helps them see the usefulness of science.

Let's look at transfer mechanisms that help students go through this process. When we have a clear understanding of how transfer occurs, we can better establish the conditions for ensuring that students meet transfer goals.

Types of Transfer: Near and Far

Science learning is cyclical, not linear, and transfer is actually happening all the time, not just at the end of a lesson or unit. In fact, the goal of *all* learning is eventual transfer (Bransford, Brown, & Cocking, 2000). By this we mean that the goals of instruction are not to leave students at the surface or even deep level, but rather to ensure that they can take what they have learned and use it in the next unit, not to mention in the next year and beyond. For example, students may learn the parts of a plant in early elementary school, the specific functions of those parts in upper elementary grades, and then transfer that learning to plant reproduction, photosynthesis, and adaptations. There is also a possibility that students will have to transfer this knowledge to areas outside of plant biology: genetics and biomedical engineering. This example represents two dimensions of transfer. To help accomplish these goals, it helps to understand that transfer actually happens across two dimensions: near transfer and far transfer (Perkins & Salomon, 1992).

Near transfer occurs when the new situation is paired closely with a context students have experienced. For example, helping students become fluent with science terminology is one of the biggest challenges elementary teachers face. What is a hypothesis? What are independent variables? Amphibians? Arachnids versus insects? Atoms, elements, and molecules? We know from experience that simply asking students to write out terms and memorize their definitions isn't very effective. If we begin by providing students with opportunities to (1) develop their own descriptions of words rather than just definitions, (2) incorporate both linguistic and nonlinguistic representations, (3) include multiple exposures to the words or concepts, (4) encourage students to discuss the words or concepts, and (5) require students to play with words (Marzano, 2004; Marzano & Pickering, 2005), this provides them with the opportunity to make sense out of what these terms mean and to use different representations to work toward understanding each term.

Video 4.1
Students as Task Managers

http://resources.corwin .com/vl-science

Let's return to Ms. Cross's classroom from Chapter 2. Learners engaged in the panther hunt activity to develop a conceptual understanding of predators, prey, food chains, and resource scarcity. When students were not able to obtain enough "food" to survive, they recognized the balance between members of an ecosystem and the factors that contribute to survival. But it didn't stop there. A few weeks later, Ms. Cross continued to develop these concepts by relating the panther hunt experience to the discussion of natural disasters and human impact on ecosystems. She had learners return to the discussion questions; for example, what would happen to the population of a species if the habitat of its prey was eliminated by a forest fire or housing development, or what would happen to this habitat if the water became polluted? Students connected the physical representation of the panther hunt to subsequent topics in life science. Ms. Cross had the goal of eventual transfer.

Later in the year, as students began to explore structural and behavioral adaptions, as well as renewable and nonrenewable resources and energy transfer in food webs, students could transfer understanding by extending their previous experiences to a new context. That is not all that was happening. Class and small-group activities that supported deep understanding of ecosystems, habitats, and food chains went on throughout the year. Discourse, both in small groups and in the whole class, is focused on looking for the relationship between living organisms, their environment, and the needs of living things. Moving back and forth among surface, deep, and transfer learning helped students become more fluent with these concepts, principles, and phenomena, as opposed to what would have happened if students were told to simply memorize definitions and facts.

The size of the leap is larger in *far transfer*, as the learner is able to make connections between more seemingly remote situations. To take the example in Chapter 3, as Mrs. Leonard engages her students in reciprocal teaching, learners begin to uncover seasonal patterns by analyzing and interpreting data related to sunrise, sunset, and seasonal patterns. Fast-forward to later grades as students are beginning to understand energy transfer between objects and within a closed system, as well as micro versus macro systems. The concept of change is an overarching idea in science that ties together life processes, physical processes, and geoscience processes. Simply telling students about the reason for the seasons provides no understanding of the dynamic change contained within living and nonliving systems. Early experiences with specific learning related to change and transformation that include surface and deep learning in Mrs. Leonard's classroom will later provide students with far transfer opportunities as they apply those understandings to dynamic processes in future science learning.

Although this approach provides us with powerful opportunities in science teaching and learning, we must be purposeful, intentional, and deliberate about how we plan and implement science learning experiences. We must ensure clarity on how scientific ideas connect to each other as lessons are planned and concepts unfold.

The Paths for Transfer: Low-Road Hugging and High-Road Bridging

If learners engage in both near and far transfer, what are mechanisms that support this path to transfer? As we create learning opportunities that support transfer, we can provide varying levels of support that are referred to as *low-road hugging* or *high-road bridging* (Perkins & Salomon, 1992). Table 4.1 summarizes each of these mechanisms and provides examples from the science classroom. The contrastive element is the extent to which the thinking involved is under the learner's conscious direction. In the left column, the teacher provides structure to support students in transfer. In the right column, the students are using their own strategies and learning to lead the work of transfer.

Let's revisit Ms. Easton's classroom from Chapter 3. As you may recall, Ms. Easton's learners were striving to explain the hierarchical structural organization of a multicellular organism and how this structure supports the essential functions of life. This strong foundation in the structure, function, and organization of multicellular organisms helps build automaticity—that is, as students continue to use this information in a variety of situations, they will reach the point where they no longer have to think about the structures and functions of the circulatory system or respiratory system. Learners simply know the essential components of the digestive system and the steps involved in the digestion of food and the absorption of the necessary nutrients for life. And because they have learned this by building on the conceptual understanding of the hierarchical structural organization of a multicellular organism and how this structure supports the essential functions of life, they not only can provide answers to questions, *Jeopardy*-style; they know when to apply this learning to different contexts, situations, and problems.

HUGGING AND BRIDGING METHODS FOR LOW-ROAD AND HIGH-ROAD TRANSFER

Hugging to Promote Low-Road Transfer	Bridging to Promote High-Road Transfer
Students are learning to apply skills and knowledge. *Students can apply what they know about the circulatory system to the oxygenation of blood.*	Students are learning to make links across concepts. *Students apply what they know about the circulatory system to aerobic exercise and the calculation of aerobic capacity.*
The teacher is associating prior knowledge with new knowledge. *The teacher provides opportunities for learners to use their prior knowledge of a pump and the function of the heart.*	A student is using multiple representations to illustrate connections across disciplines or content. *A student compares and contrasts the circulatory systems of mammals, reptiles, amphibians, birds, and/or fish.*
Students are categorizing information. *Students categorize animals based on the structure and function of their organ systems.*	Students are deriving rules and principles based on examples. *Students use this categorization to derive generalizations about species (i.e., homeostasis, warm-blooded, cold-blooded, etc.).*
The teacher asks purposeful questions. *The teacher asks students about various strategies they might use to solve a problem related to vascular disease or illnesses associated with the circulatory system.*	Students use metacognitive thinking to reflectively plan and organize. *On their own, students try various strategies to solve a problem related to disease or illness.*
Students are summarizing and rehearsing knowledge. *Students engage in a series of inquiry tasks related to red blood cells, white blood cells, and plasma and justify their thinking.*	Students are creating new and original content. *Students write their own inquiry tasks using a variety of personal contexts to apply their understanding in new situations.*

(Continued)

(Continued)

Hugging to Promote Low-Road Transfer	Bridging to Promote High-Road Transfer
The teacher creates modeling and simulation opportunities for students to apply new knowledge to parallel situations. *Students develop models of technologies that model the structures and functions of the circulatory system in animals.*	Students are applying new knowledge to dissimilar situations. *Students compare the vascular system of animals to that of plants (i.e., vascular and nonvascular plants).*

Table 4.1

Applications of this learning, such as to the regulation of homeostasis, requires higher-level thinking. Without a deeper understanding of the structure and function of specific organ systems, students would not be able to transfer learning to this new situation. Many students struggle with complex science ideas because they have not developed the conceptual understanding of ideas and they do not have the deep learning required to apply these ideas to new and more abstract situations.

We must recognize that transfer as a mechanism (1) occurs even among the youngest learners and (2) changes in appearance as the learner progresses developmentally. From Mrs. Leonard's first graders to Ms. Easton's high school biology students, learners of all ages transfer their learning as they become more independent learners. However, in science, we have to ensure that we do not overlook the unavoidable challenge of misconceptions.

Managing Misconceptions

Simply by experiencing the world around them, learners process and organize information from many sources (Rutherford & Ahlgren, 1990). As a result, they come to our science classes with already formed ideas about the world. These prior ideas are often composed of fragmented, incomplete, or naïve beliefs about scientific phenomena. The ideas are not typically consistent with accepted scientific views (Bass, Contant, & Carin, 2009). For example, learners can have misconceptions about living and nonliving things, liquids, light rays, sound, and geoscience processes. Some of the most common misconceptions are the following:

- Animals are living because they move, but plants are nonliving.
- Anything that pours is a liquid.
- When liquids evaporate, they just disappear.
- Electric current is used up in bulbs, and there is less current going back to a battery than coming out of it.
- Light rays move out from the eye in order to illuminate objects.
- Loudness and pitch are the same thing.
- Suction causes liquids to be pulled upward in a soda straw.
- The Earth is flat.
- The phases of the Moon are caused by shadows of the Earth falling on the Moon.
- Seasons are caused by the changing distance of the Earth from the Sun. (see Driver, Squires, Rushworth, & Wood-Robinson, 1994)

Within the learning process, specifically in the transfer phase, teachers must carefully monitor learners as they take the reins of their own learning, engage in metacognitive thinking, and apply what they know to a variety of real-world contexts to avoid the development of misconceptions or the self-verification of previously held misconceptions. That is, learners engaging in a transfer task might perceive the experience in a way that confirms their misconceptions instead of extracting the relevant information that aligns with accepted scientific views. By making science learning visible, teachers and learners can recognize errors in scientific reasoning and support conceptual change (Driver et al., 1994; Wandersee, Mintzes, & Novak, 1994).

Once the teacher and learners have identified a misconception or error in scientific reasoning, students must be challenged to recognize that their personal theories and scientific explanations are in conflict with scientific views. This can be done by circling back to surface-level learning through specific and targeted questioning by the teacher or direct instruction of the scientific principle. Conceptual change does not come from threatening or telling; it must engage the learner in the elaborate acquisition and consolidation of the scientific concept, as we discussed in Chapter 2. Learners then need repeated opportunities to struggle with the inconsistencies between their own ideas and accurate scientific explanations so that they can reorganize their thinking and identify the appropriate relationships (i.e., deep learning) between their own ideas and scientific concepts. Engaging in conceptual change through error recognition by the teacher and learner, followed by the return to surface- and deep-level learning, ensures that successful transfer learning can continue.

Conditions Necessary for Transfer Learning

Relevancy is a major condition for transfer learning. For learners to devote the necessary cognitive resources to transfer their learning, they must have a clear perception of what's in it for them. Learning becomes more meaningful when students see what they're learning as being meaningful in their own lives. Learning needs to have implications that are developmentally appropriate and are seen as being useful in students' learning lives. Whether near or far transfer is intended, the motivation and interest of a learner to engage in transfer depends on the context of the task. Furthermore, clear learning intentions and success criteria are essential in promoting transfer. Providing clarity on exactly what students are learning, why they are learning it, and how they know they are successful fosters transfer. Although students are engaged in more self-directed learning during this transfer period, they need goals and ways to measure their own progress to sustain engagement.

One of the problems for many students is that they rush to apply their learning to a new situation. Consider the project-learning task that requires students to construct a catapult that will project a cotton ball the furthest distance. Learners are provided with paper cups, paperclips, rubber bands, clear tape, wooden sticks, string, and a cotton ball. The mere excitement of the task motivates learners to rush into the building of a "cool" apparatus that, in the end, may or may not meet the specifications of the project-based task. Supporting students in their thinking by requiring that they pause and consider the similarities and differences between this task and other physical scenarios involving simple machines, projectile motion, and opposing forces is time well spent. Considering the specifics of the problem in front of the class, the nature of the question, and any additional details merits attention. In fact, we should model this process for learners, thinking aloud as we tackle this transfer task. Too many students, especially struggling students, jump into a new problem without thinking about how it is different from or similar to a previous problem.

A team of kindergarten teachers used an engineering design challenge to provide an opportunity for students to transfer their learning from their math, science, and literacy class to solving an authentic challenge. Given their students' fascination with certain cartoon characters who rescue or help others, these teachers provided an authentic challenge that mirrored these cartoon superheroes. These young learners were tasked with designing an object that could be pushed or pulled out of a pit using only magnets, and with presenting their object to the class. Learners were not allowed to touch the object at any time during the rescue. Teachers established small groups of students to work as design teams, or "rescue teams," across all classes; they modeled the process for working as a team to communicate effectively, establish goals, develop a timeline, and set deadlines. These team collaboration skills are essential for transfer learning and for much of authentic problem solving. Teams were provided with the following supplies: magnetic tape, cardboard, cardboard tubes, scissors, scrap paper, scrap fabric, construction paper, tape, small magnet rounds, markers, crayons, pencils, and glue. The rescue teams did not have to use all of the supplies, but they were limited to only those supplies provided to the team. By beginning with a challenge that they knew was relevant to the students, the teachers were creating prime conditions for transfer learning. The teachers' instructional intentions were to teach their students about using design thinking (Crismond & Adams, 2012) to solve a real-world problem that required application of their math, science, and literacy learning.

> Effect size for comparing and contrasting new and old problems = 1.23

While these kindergarten teachers did not teach the students *how* to solve this problem, they intentionally selected a problem that highlighted concepts students had been studying in math, science, and literacy and built on that prior knowledge in developmentally appropriate ways. The teachers knew that the students had learned to collect, organize, and analyze data.

As the rescue teams began to work, they approached the problem in different ways. Some teams sketched their design, while other teams first evaluated the strength of the magnets. Other teams used their laptops to explore different designs and evaluate the efficiency and effectiveness of these different designs. While each team had a different approach, all of them had to use their collaboration and problem-solving knowledge, along with their math, science, and literacy learning, to design a solution to the authentic problem.

The students used problem solving and reasoning to propose and test possible solutions. The practical criteria and constraints on a workable solution (e.g., the weight-bearing limits of the magnets) provided immediate and relevant feedback on potential solutions. Teachers circulated among the groups, asking questions about their strategies and helping them find effective ways to manage their sometimes conflicting ideas. Seeing the mathematics and science in this context provided opportunities for reteaching in a new way if the teachers found that students were missing requisite surface or deep knowledge. When students presented their objects and explained how each object could be rescued from the pit, teachers were given opportunities to provide feedback on literacy standards as well.

The conditions created by these kindergarten teachers allowed teams to think conceptually, especially to identify problems and propose solutions, test their proposals, make adjustments, and think of alternatives, all dispositions identified by Bereiter (2002) as evidence of transfer of learning. The teachers found a relevant and appropriate problem that built on students' prior learning. They deliberately taught teamwork skills so that students could use their reasoning skills in collaborative ways. The teachers and the problem itself provided feedback, and teachers were close at hand to reteach when necessary.

Transfer learning happens best when learners have the surface learning and deep learning necessary for transfer. When learners do not have a strong conceptual understanding or the foundational knowledge of a specific topic, transfer is not likely to happen. Keep in mind that shallow, or highly contextualized, learning will reduce the likelihood of transfer. In other words, without actively uncovering relationships among science concepts, students are unlikely to transfer. And, as mentioned previously, transfer is an active process that comes from the purposeful and intentional selection of tasks that provide learners with explicit opportunities to transfer their learning to a new context. We will examine a specific science learning task that promotes transfer learning: problem-solving teaching. Following that, we will focus on approaches that facilitate the transfer of learning in science. These include

- Communicating
- Using variables in experimentation
- Designing, constructing, and interpreting models

Selecting Science Tasks
That Promote Transfer Learning

To support the transfer of learning, teachers must select tasks that provide explicit opportunities for students to engage in authentic learning experiences. These experiences should include both low-road hugging and high-road bridging, focusing on the detection of similarities and differences among tasks or problems. Transfer learners are able to use their conceptual understanding and apply complex relationships between concepts in a new context. We have explored specific examples of transfer learning. Each of these examples exemplifies the nature of thinking. To engage in the learning expected of Mr. Ross's classroom regarding electrical circuits or the rescue teams in kindergarten, learners are using their accumulated science content knowledge and process skills and qualitatively shaping and utilizing this information in a new setting.

Transfer learning is conceptualized through the extended abstract component of the SOLO Taxonomy (Biggs & Collis, 1982). Let's continue the learning progressions from the previous chapters (Table 4.2), adding the *extended abstract* component, or transfer learning.

Again, notice the change in the level of the thinking as well as the nature of the thinking. This progression to transfer learning also provides additional opportunities to adjust the rigor of the learning experiences (see Figure 4.2).

When learners are engaged in transfer learning, ensuring that students are working on tasks that have the right level of rigor, for the right student, at the right time is essential for the successful transfer.

Consider the earlier task in which students were asked to create mass-versus-volume plots for three different substances. How could teachers adjust the difficulty and complexity of this task to provide the right level of rigor for their learners? If difficulty refers to the amount of effort a student must exert to engage in and complete a task, a teacher could provide a greater number of substances or more data points for learners to graph and analyze in order to increase the difficulty of the task.

Video 4.2
Tasks With Rigor

*http://resources.corwin
.com/vl-science*

SOLO Level	Learning Intention	Success Criteria
Uni-structural	I understand that the Earth's surface is composed of tectonic plates.	I can identify plate boundaries.
Multi-structural	I understand that certain geoscience or Earth processes occur at tectonic plate boundaries.	I can describe Earth processes that occur at tectonic plate boundaries. I can explain that certain geoscience or Earth processes occur at tectonic plate boundaries.
Relational	I understand that the type of geoscience or Earth processes depends on the movement of tectonic plates.	I can explain how the movement of tectonic plates is related to specific geoscience or Earth processes.
Extended abstract	I understand how data inform our understanding of geoscience processes.	I can utilize numerical data to describe geoscience processes. I can create a quantitative model of geoscience processes.

SOLO Level	Learning Intention	Success Criteria
Uni-structural	I understand that friction opposes motion.	I can define friction.
Multi-structural	I understand that friction occurs with both moving and stationary objects.	I can describe static and kinetic friction. I can identify examples of static and kinetic friction.
Relational	I understand that the type of friction depends on the physical characteristics of the object.	I can explain how the frictional force on an object is related to the physical characteristics of the object.
Extended abstract	I understand that the initial conditions influence how forces interact.	I can develop qualitative and quantitative models of interacting forces for various initial and boundary conditions.

Table 4.2

COMPARING DIFFICULTY AND COMPLEXITY

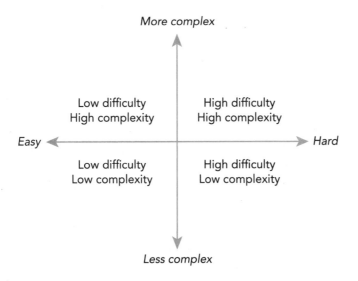

Figure 4.2

A teacher could also vary the level of difficulty by providing some learners with an already labeled graph, leaving the learner to plot the data and calculate the slope of each line. Other students may have to construct their graphs and scale the vertical and horizontal axes in addition to plotting the data and calculating the slope.

If a teacher is interested in adjusting the complexity, or the thinking involved in the task, he or she might require students to collect their data in units that must be converted. For example, the data might be in kilograms or cubic millimeters. Another example of increased complexity would be the inclusion of both pure substances and impure substances. Adding this additional variable (impurities) would require learners to increase their level of critical thinking about the procedure, data, calculations, and to develop inferences to explain the irregularities in the data.

Difficulty and complexity can be modified in STEM engineering design tasks as well. Mr. Ross could adjust the difficulty level of his resistors, insulators, and conductors task by providing learners with visual schematics that still require that learners assemble the electronic devices and justify their decisions, but not yet necessitate that they be fluent in the terminology associated with electrical circuits. In addition, opportunities to research specific electrical devices could be made available to those learners who need to enhance their familiarity with certain components or devices. This specific group of learners may be ready to engage in the complexity of reconstructing electrical devices, but at a different level of difficulty. The difficulty of this task could be increased by providing more components and more devices that need to be assembled. The students would need to deal with a greater quantity of components, but the level of thinking would be the same. One final example is the familiarity of the devices. To enhance the difficulty, Mr. Ross could select devices that the students are not familiar with, so that they must focus on additional characteristics of the components. This also leads to increased complexity. Providing parts that are not associated with any of the disassembled devices would require learners to evaluate each item to decide not only which device the component is associated with, but also whether the component is necessary at all.

A similar set of adjustments in complexity and difficulty could be made to the magnet rescue activity in the kindergarten classroom. Adjusting the physical characteristics of the pit, providing visual examples, and supplying different strengths of magnets changes the difficulty of the rescue mission. Providing more materials, including materials that are not useful at all, or creating a dynamic environment (i.e., with sand, soil, or water) manipulates the complexity by providing additional variables and interactions in the design challenge.

The decision to adjust the difficulty and/or complexity of any task rests solely on the readiness of the learners. This, of course, comes from formative assessment data that make student learning and thinking visible to both the teacher and the students. What is important to note in each of these scenarios is that adjusting the difficulty of a specific activity ensures that all learners have access to complex thinking, regardless of their background or prior experiences. English language learners should not be inhibited from engaging in transfer learning simply because they are developing proficiency in language. In this case, adjusting the difficulty of a task, leaving the complexity constant, provides a more inclusive visible science learning environment. Similarly, learners with special needs can engage in the same level of complex thinking as their peers when barriers to engaging in that thinking are removed from the task. This is done by changing the difficulty of a task, not the complexity.

Finally, learners who need to be challenged in their thinking benefit from increasing the complexity but maintaining an ideal level of difficulty. We do not want learners with a proclivity for science to avoid a challenge because they equate it with more work.

Helping Students Transform Scientific Understanding

Problem-Solving Teaching

In the previous chapter, we discussed the use of inquiry-based teaching and how that specific approach was successful in scaffolding deep learning. Within science education, problem-based learning (PBL) is commonly presented as an effective approach for the teaching and learning of science. The successful implementation of both approaches, as well as direct instruction, highlights the challenge of science teachers in not just identifying what works, as almost everything works for some students at some time, especially when zero growth is expected. Instead, we need to match what works to accelerate student learning, and then implement it at the right time (Hattie, 2009). PBL is one such practice. The evidence indicates that when PBL is used too early in the learning cycle, before students have had sufficient experience with the required surface learning, the effect size is very low: 0.15. Without a strong foundational and conceptual understanding of science content and process skills, learners are not equipped with enough knowledge to pursue this level of inquiry. But when *problem-solving teaching* is used during the transfer phase of learning, not PBL, the effect size skyrockets. Unlike conventional PBL, where the problem is presented to students in advance of knowledge acquisition, problem-solving teaching is deployed when students are already deepening their knowledge.

Video 4.3
Transferring Scientific Processes to Science Learning

http://resources.corwin .com/vl-science

Problem-solving teaching is distinct from the problem-solving process. Problem solving in this broad sense involves

Effect size for problem-solving teaching = 0.68

- Defining or determining the cause of the problem
- Using multiple perspectives to uncover issues related to a particular problem
- Identifying, prioritizing, and selecting alternatives for a solution
- Designing an intervention plan
- Evaluating the outcome (Hattie, 2009, p. 210)

Problem-solving teaching helps students engage in the process of determining the cause of a problem; using multiple perspectives to uncover issues; identifying, prioritizing, and selecting alternatives for a solution; designing an intervention plan; and evaluating the outcome.

STEM activities, in the form of engineering design challenges (Hester & Cunningham, 2007), are one form of problem-solving teaching that can encourage the transfer of science learning to mathematics, literacy, social studies, and the arts. In an engineering design challenge, students are asked to craft a solution to a problem within a set of criteria (the way we measure success) and constraints (limitations on the resources we can use). This requires learners to make connections between the elements of the design challenge (problem) and the science and other disciplinary knowledge they bring to finding an optimal solution. For example, learners in Mrs. Snyder's fifth-grade classroom wonder about the relationship between solar energy and the reflectivity and thermal conductivity of materials. Mrs. Snyder provides her learners with the STEM design challenge of developing a solar cooker that would melt a marshmallow (adapted from www.childrensengineering.org). The only requirements placed on the solar cookers are that the cookers must be freestanding, hold a thermometer, and easily hold a large marshmallow. Collaborative learning teams are allowed to use any materials they feel would help them solve the design challenge. However, they have to defend their choice of materials.

Mrs. Snyder's fifth graders engage in an iterative process to develop their solar cookers, a process with several components. Notice the similarities to the previously described problem-solving teaching approach:

1. Define the problem by asking questions about the situation.
2. Explore the elements of the problem, imagine potential solutions, and develop a plan.
3. Make and test a model or prototype.
4. Reflect on the testing and identify improvements to your solution. Revise/retest the plan.

This iterative process can continue as long as time and resources permit. Teachers can often identify design challenges for their students by listening thoughtfully to their wondering about the world around them. As in the earlier example, kindergarten students might wonder about the strength of magnets and how to best leverage magnetic fields to move objects. Learners in an elementary classroom might wonder about which fruits and vegetables grow best in the local soil and climate. By high school, student wonderings are often connected to the problems they will solve as adults or that will provide a service to the rest of the world. For example, Mr. Martin's environmental science class developed protocols for water filtration systems that could be used in unindustrialized nations.

Scientific Processes and Thinking

Just as learners transfer science content to new contexts, scenarios, or problems, they also engage in scientific processes that support this type of thinking. Referring back to Chapter 2: As learners become more proficient at making observations, assimilating observations from various perspectives or sources, and using data generated from observations to formulate questions in the classroom, they have developed the foundational skills necessary to work in dynamic situations that require them to make decisions similar to those involved in practicing science. This is the transfer of observational skills from the controlled laboratory to the field. For example, learners might now be asked not only to make observations in a specific habitat, but also to be able to select the specific methodology and instruments for making observations unique to that habitat, which generates relevant and useable data for answering a scientific question. The difference lies in the specific environment, or context, in which students make these observations. In a controlled laboratory setting (i.e., the classroom), teachers can limit the number of variables or possible sources or error in a given situation. Determining the population density of a specific organism in a well-controlled laboratory experiment is far different from working out in the field in a dynamic ecosystem, battling the elements in a flowing stream. Collecting data on subatomic particles through an experiment in your high school astronomy class is very different from collecting data from the Great Canary Telescope in Spain.

The transfer of process skills, like making observations, requires that learners incorporate the uncertainty inherent in the nature of science. This uncertainty lies in the dynamic and complex nature of scientific phenomena, the limitations of scientific instrumentation, and the potential for error in measurement. For science learners to successfully navigate this intrinsic characteristic of science, they must have a strong conceptual understanding of what it means to engage in scientific observation as well as the relationship between observations, data, and scientific questioning. As with science content knowledge, this transfer must be taught. Table 4.3 follows this progression from the previous two chapters, presenting the learning intention and success criteria for this next step in the progression: extended abstract, or transfer.

SOLO Level	Learning Intention	Success Criteria
Uni-structural	I understand that the characteristics of objects are identified by direct observation.	I can identify the properties of an object by using my senses.
Multi-structural	I understand that observations can be made from multiple perspectives.	I can describe an object from different positions. I can identify differences in an object from different perspectives.
Relational	I understand that observations provide data for developing scientific questions.	I can relate my predictions and scientific questions to specific observations. I can describe the relationship between observing and formulating questions.
Extended abstract	I understand that observations are limited by the nature of the instruments used and the error associated with those instruments.	I can evaluate the reliability and validity of my observations. I can explain the limitations and potential sources of error in my observations.

Table 4.3

What is important to note here is that learning to "do" science, or to engage in the processes of science, requires that learners move through the learning process from surface, to deep, to transfer. In the previous two chapters, we focused on specific processes as mere examples of what this progression would look like in the classroom. With that being said, here are examples of the learning progression for the process skills of:

- Communicating
- Using variables in experimentation
- Designing, constructing, and interpreting models

For communication, notice how the learners progress from building a conceptual understanding of what it means to communicate in science to the relationship between communicating and other scientific processes. Finally, learners are expected to transfer this learning to reviewing

PROCESS PROGRESSION CHART FOR COMMUNICATING

1. Observations are recorded, and picture graphs are constructed.

2. Objects are described both pictorially and verbally.

3. Observations and data are recorded, analyzed, and communicated orally and with simple graphs, pictures, written statements, and numbers.

4. Data are collected and recorded, and bar graphs are constructed using numbered axes.

5. Observations and data are communicated.

6. Data are gathered, charted, graphed, and analyzed.

7. Data are collected, recorded, analyzed, and communicated using proper graphical representations and metric measurements.

8. Data are organized into tables showing repeated trials and means.

9. Data are organized, communicated through graphical representation, interpreted, and used to make predictions.

10. Numbers are expressed in scientific notation where appropriate.

(Continued)

(Continued)

11. Data tables showing the independent and dependent variables, derived quantities, and the number of trials are constructed and interpreted. Data tables for descriptive statistics showing specific measures of central tendency, the range of the data set, and the number of repeated trials are constructed and interpreted.

12. Experimental results are presented in appropriate written form.

13. Appropriate technology, including computers, graphing calculators, and probeware, is used for gathering and analyzing data, communicating results, modeling concepts, and simulating experimental conditions.

14. Research utilizes scientific literature.

15. A scientific viewpoint is constructed and defended.

16. A description of a physical, authentic, or real-world problem is translated into a mathematical statement in order to find a solution. (adapted from VDOE, 2012)

appropriate scientific literature, selecting the most appropriate medium for communication, translating the scientific problem into a mathematical statement, and then, finally, constructing and defending a scientific viewpoint.

This same progression is found in each scientific process: from surface, to deep, to transfer. Looking at the Commonwealth of Virginia's intentional and purposeful development of the progressions for each process skill, some of the skills are not introduced until second or third grade (see Figure 4.3). At that time, the learner is more likely to have the surface learning necessary to design, construct, and interpret models, for example.

We have highlighted the progression of specific process skills through learning intentions and success criteria. These process skills must be taught. However, they should not be taught in isolation; instead, they should be embedded with content. Observing, communicating,

COMMONWEALTH OF VIRGINIA'S DEVELOPMENT OF PROGRESSIONS FOR PROCESS SKILLS

Introduction[1] Proficiency Advanced Mastery

	GRADE/COURSE										
	2	3	4	5	6	LS	PS	ES	BI	CH	PH
DESIGNING, CONSTRUCTING, AND INTERPRETING MODELS											
Simple physical models are designed and constructed to clarify explanations and show relationships. (2.11)											
Models are designed and built. (3.11)		1									
Models are constructed to clarify explanations, demonstrate relationships, and solve needs. (4.11)											
Models are constructed to clarify explanations, demonstrate relationships, and solve needs. (5.1j)											
Scale models are used to estimate distance, volume, and quantity. (6.1c)											
Models and simulations are designed and used to illustrate and explain phenomena and systems. (6.1i)											
Models and simulations are constructed and used to illustrate and explain phenomena. (LS.1d)											
Models and simulations are constructed and used to illustrate and explain phenomena. (PS.1m)											
Technologies, including computers, probeware, and geospatial technologies, are used to collect, analyze, and report data and to demonstrate concepts and simulate experimental conditions. (ES.1b) (Communicating, Analyzing Data)*											
Maps and globes are read and interpreted, including location by latitude and longitude. (ES.1d)											
Appropriate technology, including computers, graphing calculators, and probeware, is used for gathering and analyzing data, communicating results, modeling concepts, and simulating experimental conditions. (BIO.1i) (Communicating, Analyzing Data)											
Alternative scientific explanations and models are recognized and analyzed. (BIO.11) (Analyzing Data)									2		
Use of appropriate technology, including computers, graphing calculators, and probeware, for gathering data, communicating results, and using simulations to model concepts. (CH.1h) (Communicating)											
Models and simulations are used to visualize and explain phenomena, to make predications from hypotheses, and to interpret data. (PH.1f) (Analyzing Data)											

1. Proficient performance on an introduced skill in routine classroom tasks and performances is expected by the end of grade-level/course instruction unless indicated by multiple introductory year blocks.

2. The Computer Technology SOL introduces the use of hand-held technologies in the middle grades, e.g., C/T 6-8.6 and 6-8.8.

* When a skill is repeated, the additional location is indicated by parentheses.

Source: Adapted from VDOE (2012).

Figure 4.3

PROCESS PROGRESSION CHART FOR USING VARIABLES IN EXPERIMENTATION

1. Simple investigations and experiments are conducted to answer questions.

2. Conditions that influence a change are identified, and inferences are made.

3. Independent and dependent variables are identified.

4. Constants in an experimental situation are identified.

5. One variable is manipulated over time, using many repeated trials.

6. Sources of experimental error are identified.

7. Dependent variables, independent variables, and constants are identified.

8. Variables are controlled to test hypotheses, and trials are repeated.

9. Independent and dependent variables, constants, controls, and repeated trials are identified.

10. Research methods are used to investigate practical problems and questions.

11. Variables are manipulated with repeated trials.

12. Variables are defined, and investigations are designed to test hypotheses.

13. Sources of error inherent in experimental design are identified and discussed.

14. Designated laboratory techniques are implemented.

15. Verifiable observations and data are obtained through the manipulation of multiple variables, using repeated trials.

16. The limitations of the experimental apparatus and design are recognized. (adapted from VDOE, 2012)

PROCESS PROGRESSION CHART FOR DESIGNING, CONSTRUCTING, AND INTERPRETING MODELS

1. Simple physical models are designed and constructed to clarify explanations and show relationships.

2. Models are designed and built.

3. Models are constructed to clarify explanations, demonstrate relationships, and solve needs.

4. Scale models are used to estimate distance, volume, and quantity.

5. Models and simulations are designed and used to illustrate and explain phenomena and systems.

6. Models and simulations are constructed and used to illustrate and explain phenomena.

7. Technologies, including computers, probeware, and geospatial technologies, are used to collect, analyze, and report data and to demonstrate concepts and simulate experimental conditions.

8. Maps and globes are read and interpreted, including location by latitude and longitude.

9. Alternative scientific explanations and models are recognized and analyzed.

10. Models and simulations are used to visualize and explain phenomena, to make predictions from hypotheses, and to interpret data. (adapted from VDOE, 2012)

interpreting, analyzing, and evaluating data; using variables; and constructing models should be a part of the learning experience in the classrooms of Ms. Cross, Mr. Patterson, Mr. Smith, and all the other teachers highlighted in this book. Actively engaging learners in content and process skills allows thinking to become visible, opening the door to better opportunities for feedback. What we will discuss next is that the progression from surface to deep to transfer includes self-regulation feedback. The learner moves closer and closer to taking the reins of his or her own learning, even his or her own feedback.

Feedback

As is the case with surface and deep learning, students need specific, constructive, and timely feedback that provides vital information about where they are going, how they are going there, and where they are going next. Through self-regulation feedback, learners know what to do, when they don't know what to do, and the teacher is not available. Transfer learning is accompanied by self-regulation feedback, although self-regulation feedback is not the only type of feedback that is important in transfer learning. For example, when a misconception arises or a gap in surface learning is detected, learners benefit from both task and process feedback. However, a majority of the feedback at this part of the learning process should be self-regulation through metacognition.

When learners practice metacognition through self-verbalization, self-questioning, and self-reflection, they take personal ownership of their learning, which provides increased motivation and understanding. This is a well-documented finding in education research (e.g., National Research Council, 2007). Metacognition, or the ability to think about your own thinking, promotes learners' awareness of themselves, the task at hand, and what they need to do to successfully complete the task. Again, put another way, learners know what to do when they don't know what to do and the teacher is not available. This is self-regulation feedback. Metacognitive processes have been shown quite clearly to boost student achievement. Marzano (1998, p. 106) called metacognition the "engine" that drives thinking. Palincsar (2013) describes metacognitive awareness as consisting of three parts:

1. Knowledge about our learning selves
2. An understanding of what the task demands and necessary strategies to complete it
3. The means to monitor learning and self-regulate

For science, this means that the learners have clear knowledge about where they are in their own learning about, say, atmospheric characteristics of the inner and outer planets. Furthermore, learners know what is expected of them in a specific task focusing on the planets and what strategies to select to meet the learning intention and success criteria. Finally, students then monitor their own progress toward the specific learning intention and success criteria. Yet students need scaffolding as they progress toward this metacognitive awareness. To develop their metacognitive skills, students need to learn the art of self-questioning.

Self-Verbalization and Self-Questioning

Learners can and do engage in self-verbalizing and self-questioning at all stages of learning. However, to effectively use this metacognitive strategy, they must have both the surface learning and the deep learning required to formulate questions and internal responses that move them closer to successful learning. This is, of course, transfer learning. Take, for example, Mr. Ross's learners and their disassembled electronic devices. As each collaborative group moves through this task, they are most successful when they think about their own thinking. They must engage in self-verbalizing and self-questioning that detects errors in their process and also justifies the decisions they believe to be a successful approach to solving the problem. Specifically, they may realize that they've reached a dead end with their approach to matching electronic components with the specific electronic device or that they are missing an important piece of information. These realizations come from a background series of questions we continually ask ourselves: *Does this make sense? Am I making progress toward finding a solution?* This self-questioning is a critical element of our metacognition, as it allows us to track our understanding and catch ourselves when we realize that we are off target.

Self-questioning is a metacognitive strategy that allows learners to track their understanding and provide themselves with self-regulation feedback when they are off target. When learners engage in self-questioning and the teacher monitors this self-questioning, error detection, or the likelihood that we will catch misconceptions, increases with each learner. In these cases, rather than simply providing task feedback (e.g., right or wrong) to the learner, the teacher and the learner can collaboratively engage in self-questioning to provide the feedback needed to get the learner back on target. This modeling of self-questioning with the teacher provides additional scaffolding as learners become more metacognitive.

> Effect size for self-verbalization and self-questioning = 0.55

How can teachers get their science learners to think about their own thinking? Hastie (2011) found success by having mathematics teachers administer quick pre-lesson and post-lesson questions that encouraged metacognition (see Figure 4.4). Not only did the students learn more math; they also showed higher levels of motivation and attention. This strategy does not have to be isolated to mathematics teaching and learning. The same deliberate and intentional process can and should be used in the science classroom. The main idea behind this approach is that teachers must help learners become more metacognitive. If learners are expected to engage in transfer learning—to take the reins of their own learning—they must think about their own thinking. Through this thinking, they should be able to monitor both their thoughts and progress toward the learning intention and success criteria. This, of course, is self-regulation feedback.

Hastie's results were quite impressive, though teachers will want to alter the checklist options based on their students and the specific lesson. For example, having students provide evidence that they did or did not meet the learning target makes their thinking visible, allowing both the teacher and the students to see where additional surface or deep learning is needed for the next day. Or, teachers could use this approach to co-construct success criteria and the evidence students would generate to show their progress toward a particular learning intention. As young learners engage in the science tasks for the day, they can constantly self-verbalize and self-question whether their work aligns with the success criteria they helped establish at the beginning of the class. Presenting this information as a checklist is compelling because students can make checkmarks on a list pretty quickly, so you can bank more time for collaborative learning and rich class discussions.

There is also something about writing that clarifies students' understanding, though. Integrating writing into the science classroom makes learners better writers by providing an authentic context for which writing is necessary in today's world. It also helps them clarify their own understanding of the science itself. As many students have told us, "We didn't know what we thought until we wrote it down."

Ms. Allen integrates writing instruction into her middle school science classroom. In addition to having her learners transfer their science learning by developing argumentative essays about a specific scientific or environmental viewpoint, informative research reports about topics under investigation, and nonfiction narratives that explain a complex science phenomenon to those in the community, she also uses writing to engage

PRE-LESSON AND POST-LESSON QUESTIONS FOR SELF-VERBALIZATION AND SELF-QUESTIONING

- What are today's goals?

- How much do I already know about today's goals? ("Nothing" to "A great deal")

- I think today's goal will be . . . ("Very hard" to "Very easy")

At the end of a lesson, students would answer questions such as the following:

- What was today's goal?

- Did I achieve this goal? ("Not at all" to "Fully")

- How much effort did I put in? ("Not much" to "A great deal")

Then the students had a chance to think about why they may or may not have achieved their goals. They could tick off the reasons from options such as the following:

- I wanted to learn about today's lesson.

- I wanted to achieve today's goal.

- I paid attention, etc.

Or . . .

- I gave up.

- It was too hard.

- I didn't understand what I was supposed to be doing, etc.

Figure 4.4

her learners in metacognition. At the beginning of a lesson, Ms. Allen uses prompts to ask students to write in their interactive science notebooks:

- How much do I already know about today's learning intention? What makes me say that?

- How difficult do I think this lesson will be? Why do I think that?

- How do I rate my desire to be successful in this lesson? Why do I want to be successful?

- How much effort will I put into today's lesson?
- What strategies do I think will be helpful for me in meeting my learning objective today?

Ms. Allen decides which questions will be the most useful based on her ongoing evaluation of student cognition, metacognition, and attitudes toward learning. She also thinks about how much class time she wants to spend on this part of the lesson. At several points during Ms. Allen's lessons, she has her students pause from the science instruction and rate their understanding of the learning intention again, and have them explain why they gave themselves their ratings. This leads to some interesting student writing, as they reflect, analyze, and clarify for themselves their levels of understanding. It also helps keep Ms. Allen's learners focused on the learning intentions and success criteria as they note their progress.

Self-Reflection

Successful learners not only question themselves; they also think about the answers to those questions and change their strategies and routines based on what most leads them to success. Self-reflection is a follow-up technique once a lesson has occurred that helps students understand where they were and where they are now. This self-reflection allows learners to develop expertise and avoid making the same errors multiple times when engaged in future tasks related to similar science content or process skills. Once Ms. Allen's students are done with the majority of the lesson, she asks them to reflect on their experience. Figure 4.5 includes some of her go-to prompts for facilitating her students' reflections and metacognitive awareness.

As the year progresses, learners become more self-aware in their learning, and by the end of the first term, these learners are engaging in self-regulation feedback, simply because they are thinking about their own thinking within the context of what they are learning in Ms. Allen's classroom. Again, they are taking the reins of their own learning.

Conclusion

Transfer is the goal of science teaching and learning. When learners first develop a strong foundational and conceptual understanding of science content knowledge and process skills, they begin to make generalizations and connections across various topics. Making connections between the

PROMPTS FOR FACILITATING STUDENTS' SELF-REFLECTION AND METACOGNITIVE AWARENESS

- How well do I think I understand _____ now?
- Why do I think that?
- How has my understanding increased as a result of today's lesson?
- What questions do I still have about the science I learned today?
- What do I still need to work on? How do I know?
- How do I rate my effort during today's lesson? Why?
- How do I rate my teamwork today? Why?
- Did I ask for help? Did I offer to help others? Did I encourage my teammates?
- How did I contribute to my group's efforts?
- If I could do _____ over again, what would I do differently? Why?
- What advice would I have for another student who was about to start this same lesson?

Figure 4.5

weather patterns, climate, soil composition, and processes necessary for plants to survive and adapt in an environment paves the way for a learner to transfer this learning to the agricultural economies of ancient civilizations and the role these economies played in conflicts among those civilizations. However, this process requires the development and implementation of tasks that foster and nurture transfer learning. In addition to the theme of this book—that each phase of learning requires that the learning be visible to both the teacher and the student—we also want to emphasize that transfer learning is accessible to all learners, regardless of their individual characteristics. Whether learners are expected to transfer science learning to the next topic in the curriculum, develop scientific literacy, or engage in the development of innovations that solve tomorrow's challenges, creating a learning environment that supports this type of thinking is necessary and vital in terms of whether or not we reach the goal of transfer.

Reflection Questions

1. What does transfer look like in your classroom? Where in your classroom are students expected to engage in near transfer? Where are students expected to engage in far transfer? How do you support this part of the learning process?

2. How do you determine when your learners are progressing to transfer learning? What evidence do you collect? Do you share this evidence with your learners? Why or why not?

3. Consider the use of problem-solving teaching, contrasting cases, and analogies in your classroom. How would you adjust the difficulty of those tasks to ensure that all learners have access to complex thinking? When might you adjust the complexity of the task? What are some specific examples?

4. How do you support learners' metacognition? What is the role of self-regulation in your classroom? How do you teach learners to engage in self-verbalization, self-questioning, and self-reflection? How could you make this an essential part of the science teaching and learning in your classroom?

SCIENCE LEARNING MADE VISIBLE THROUGH EVALUATION

5

Ms. Chloe has designed a learning task that will allow her students to develop an understanding of the relationship between an object, its shadow, and the light source. She opens the lesson by identifying background knowledge about the sun and shadows. During the class's morning meeting, she shows her students several images of shadows, and she demonstrates shadows, eliciting student ideas through direct questioning. Learners are given multiple opportunities to think-pair-share with their shoulder partners. Students then work at various centers, investigating the relationships between the object, the object's position, the light source, and the shadows. Finally, learners transition outside to transfer this learning to objects in nature.

This learning task incorporates classroom discussion, inquiry, and then problem-solving teaching. Ms. Chloe will provide an engaging task that offers her young learners opportunities to build conceptual understanding, discover connections, and then transfer their learning to a new context. However, the success of this learning relies on Ms. Chloe's careful evaluation of her students' progress in their learning.

> Effect size for formative evaluation = 0.90

The evaluation of learning is the final and essential component in making science learning visible.

Determining Impact

Video 5.1
Determining Your Impact

http://resources.corwin.com/vl-science

Visible learning happens when teachers see learning through the eyes of their students and students see themselves as their own teachers. In practice, this requires that teachers are constantly evaluating their impact on student learning so that they can truly see learning through the eyes of their students. Furthermore, students must have clear knowledge about their own learning so that they can be active in the learning process, plan the next steps, and understand what is behind the assessment. The metric utilized in visible learning research is the effect size, or the quantitative measure of growth. The effect size of 0.40 (calculated with Cohen's *d*) indicates that students have gained at least a year's worth of growth for a year in school. The implication is that 0.40 should be the expectation for instruction and intervention. An effect size *lower* than 0.40 suggests that the instruction or intervention was less than effective and may warrant change or revision. At the very minimum, an effect size below 0.40 begs for a discussion about the effort.

Calculating effect size and using this tool to evaluate growth can be applied to your science classroom. Teachers can calculate effect sizes for their classes and individual students to determine the impact of their science instruction and, when necessary, the interventions needed to support students at different locations in the learning process. Understanding this impact for a particular topic or unit of study, instead of waiting for the end-of-course assessment, provides a clearer picture of overall student progress and allows for a more responsive and proactive approach to teaching and learning. Put differently, teachers and learners can make the necessary changes to the learning process when that learning is visible beyond a single, standardized measure.

Determining impact builds teachers' sense of efficacy, which is the belief in their ability to positively impact student learning. Jerald (2007) noted that teachers with strong self-efficacy

- Tend to exhibit greater levels of planning and organization
- Are more open to new ideas and are more willing to experiment with new methods to better meet the needs of their students
- Are more persistent and resilient when things do not go smoothly
- Are less critical of students when they make errors
- Are less inclined to refer a difficult student to special education (Protheroe, 2008, p. 43).

Teachers can calculate effect sizes for their classes and individual students to determine the impact their instruction and intervention have had. Student learning at the classroom level can be held to the same standard that researchers use: an effect size of at least 0.40. The process of calculating an effect size is fairly simple. Over time, as teachers discuss the data and success with their peers, they develop collective teacher efficacy ($ES = 1.57$). Goddard, Hoy, and Hoy (2000) define *collective teacher efficacy* as "the perceptions of teachers in a school that the efforts of the faculty as a whole will have a positive effect on students" (p. 480), with teachers agreeing that "teachers in this school can get through to the most difficult students" (p. 480). Importantly, perceptions are formed based on our experiences. When teachers experience success in collaborating with peers and when those collaborations improve teaching and learning, the teachers notice the results. These accumulated data points become the collective efficacy that researchers note as so powerful in student learning (Hoy, Sweetland, & Smith, 2002). Successful schools include both successful teachers and a focus on student learning.

Calculating the Effect Size

To calculate the effect size, we must have pre-assessment data and post-assessment data. Mr. Klein's chemistry class has just submitted individual laboratory reports for their acid-base titration laboratory, during which they calculated the concentration of an unknown liquid. This is the second laboratory report his learners have submitted this semester. He is interested in measuring his class's overall growth in writing laboratory reports as well as individual student growth. Table 5.1 contains the laboratory report rubric scores from his first-period class. Mr. Klein uses a 7-point rubric so that he can provide more precise information for students about their development in the writing of laboratory reports. The rubric includes descriptors for the traits of context or introduction, methodology, experimental error, data presentation, data analysis, scientific writing, and organization.

To calculate an effect size, you would first determine the average for the posttest and the average for the pretest laboratory scores. It's easy to do this in an Excel spreadsheet, which we have set up and provided for you on the book's companion website.

In Mr. Klein's classroom, the average pre-assessment score was 3.74. After a month of work on scientific writing, the students in Mr. Klein's class increased to an average of 4.69, or 1 point on the 7-point rubric. To determine whether this is an impact that is less than, equal to, or greater than one year's worth of growth, Mr. Klein will have to look beyond the 1-point change on the rubric. A 1-point average growth doesn't sound very impressive, so Mr. Klein needs to calculate the effect size. The next step in determining the effect size is to calculate standard deviation. Again, this is modeled for you in the online resources for this book, on the companion website. From there, Mr. Klein can calculate the effect size by using the following formula:

$$\text{Effect size} = \frac{\text{Average (post-assessment)} - \text{Average (pre-assessment)}}{\text{Average standard deviation, or } SD}$$

The standard deviation for Mr. Klein's first laboratory report, or the pre-assessment in this scenario, is 0.74, and the standard deviation

STUDENT LABORATORY REPORT SCORES

Name	Pre-Assessment	Post-Assessment	Individual Effect Size
Justin	3.5	4.5	1.13
Laura	2.5	3	0.56
Madison	4	4.5	0.56
Danielle	4	5.5	1.69
Lexi	3.5	5	1.69
Samantha	4	6	2.26
Lauren	4	5	1.13
Karla	5	6	1.13
Kimberly	4	3.5	−0.56
Ingrid	4	4.5	0.56
Juliana	3.5	5	1.69
Amanda	1.5	1.5	0.00
Samantha	3	3.5	0.56
Caroline	3.5	5	1.69
Erin	5	5.5	0.56
Isabel	3.5	4	0.56
Christiana	3	4	1.13
Dori	4.5	5.5	1.13
KellyAnne	3.5	5	1.69
Alice	3.5	3	−0.56
Sarah	3.5	5	1.69
Dana	4	5	1.13
Bridgett	5	5.5	0.56
Ronald	4.5	6	1.69
Sam	4	6	2.26
Mary	3	5	2.26
Jenna	3.5	4	0.56
Bryce	4.5	5.5	1.13

(Continued)

Name.	Pre-Assessment	Post-Assessment	Individual Effect Size
Joey	4	5	1.13
Danny	3	4	1.13
Lindsey	4	5	1.13
Average point score	3.74	4.69	
Standard deviation	0.74	1.03	
Average standard deviation	0.89		
Average effect size	1.08		

Table 5.1

for the second laboratory report, or post-assessment is 1.03. Therefore, the average of the two is 0.89. When the effect size is calculated using the formula above, it comes to 1.08, which is above the threshold of 0.40. Thus, Mr. Klein can conclude that his efforts to improve his students' scientific writing skills were successful. He can then infer that the focus on the processes of science associated with acid-base reactions and how to present scientific ideas in writing worked. However, keep in mind that effect sizes do not establish causation. Mr. Klein cannot say with confidence that specific actions within his instruction caused this improvement in laboratory writing; however, he should be encouraged to share his approach with others so that they can determine the impact it might have on their students.

Once Mr. Klein has the average effect size for the entire class, he can calculate the individual effect size for each student. This will allow him to further unpack the learning progress of each individual's scientific writing and, as we will discuss next, provide the necessary support and scaffolding for learners who did not respond to instruction of this skill as well as other learners did. To calculate effect sizes for individual students, Mr. Klein would use the following formula:

$$\text{Effect size} =$$

$$\frac{\text{Individual score (post-assessment)} - \text{Individual score (pre-assessment)}}{\text{Average standard deviation, or } SD \text{ for the class}}$$

Selecting Evaluations That Promote Visible Science Learning

Although it may sound redundant, evaluations that promote visible science learning are evaluations that make student thinking visible. There is a time and place for true/false and multiple-choice questions, but they often do not provide insight into student thinking. In most cases, we know only that the student selected the correct response, without gaining any information about the thinking process utilized to choose that answer. Plus, as demonstrated by the example from Mr. Klein's chemistry class, measuring student growth is just as possible with tasks or evaluations such as student laboratory reports as it is with true/false or multiple-choice questions. To ensure that the evaluation of learning provides the insight necessary to make the best decisions about where to go next, teachers and learners most benefit from tasks that make thinking visible. This includes evaluations that

Video 5.2
Continual Assessment

*http://resources.corwin
.com/vl-science*

1. Provide opportunities for learners to describe and observe what they see, not simply give definitions

2. Create learning tasks that ask students to build explanations and interpretations of scientific phenomena

3. Encourage students to not just answer questions but also to reason and justify their responses with evidence

4. Engage learners in tasks that require them to take different perspectives or viewpoints

5. Ask learners to explicitly make connections

6. Provide a space for learners to pose additional questions or wonders about the world around them

7. Conclude learning experiences by asking learners to articulate the big idea behind their learning

8. Offer opportunities for learners to uncover the complexities of scientific phenomena (adapted from Ritchhart, Church, & Morrison, 2011)

From these tasks and evaluations, teachers and learners can extract the necessary pre-assessment data and post-assessment data and monitor the learning progress between these two points.

Pre-Assessment

Without a pre-assessment of learners' content knowledge and process skills in science, we cannot determine whether learning occurred within a specific topic or unit of study. When teachers use only post-assessments, such as end-of-unit tests, essays, or projects, they will know who has demonstrated the expected level of achievement (and who has not), but they won't know who has demonstrated growth in their learning. This can be problematic, given that Graham Nuthall's research (2007) suggests that students already know 60% of what we expect them to learn. Measuring growth is paramount if we are have the greatest impact on our learners.

We often overlook the pre-assessment and believe that summative assessments mean that learning has occurred. Those data indicate that learning has occurred at some time but do not provide evidence that the learning occurred as a result of the most immediate set of experiences. This is understandable in the age of accountability. However, without pre-assessment, becoming a better teacher and designer of high-impact learning situations is left to chance. Failing to identify what students know and can do at the outset of a unit of study blocks any ability to determine whether learning has occurred and thus any ability for there to be a discussion about effective instruction and intervention. Armed with baseline, pre-assessment information, teachers can design instructional interventions to close the gap between what students already know and what they are expected to learn. In this case, time is used more precisely because specific strategies can be selected based on the type of learning needed: surface, deep, or transfer. Students who have a need for surface-level learning are probably not going to do well with a series of problem-solving teaching lessons. On the other hand, students who need deep learning are probably not going to benefit from learning mnemonics. Evaluating learning is essential in this process.

Post-Assessment

If learning is change, the post-assessment helps us measure that change after learning a specific topic or completing a unit of study. To capture this growth, teachers now must provide a post-assessment that is either the same as the pre-assessment or one that measures exactly the same content or skills and understandings. For example, Mr. Klein did not ask his students to write the same laboratory report for the same experiment when administering his post-assessment. Instead, he asked his learners to utilize the same skills and understandings to engage in scientific writing. On the other hand, content-focused learning may be best measured using the same pre-assessment measure. This opens the door to an investigation about impact. Did learners grow, or learn, over the period of time between these two evaluations?

When the pre- and posttest data are available, the effect size can be determined. Table 5.1 previously modeled how this would look in Mr. Klein's classroom. What is most important here is not necessarily the set of numbers, but what we do with those numbers. These numbers account for what learners already knew, were proficient in, or had mastered prior to the learning. What about learners who made significant gains—gains greater than 0.40, or the target effect size threshold? What about learners who made a gain of exactly 0.40? Finally, what about learners who did not make a gain of at least 0.40?

Mr. Klein, or any teacher who measures his or her impact by looking at growth, can make intentional and purposeful decisions about where to go next with learners. The teacher can decide how to adjust the difficulty or complexity of the next learning experience based on gaps in student learning. This could be done by adjusting the difficulty or complexity of the subsequent tasks, as well as by providing small-group or individual interventions for those who need different levels of support and scaffolding.

Response to Intervention in the Science Classroom

Sometimes, despite our best efforts, students fail to respond to high-quality science instruction. Whether students are tasked with making conversions in the metric system, calculating the density of a substance, or determining the molarity of a solution, learners will progress at different rates in their science learning. Awareness of each learner's progress through the formative evaluation ($ES = 0.68$) better positions teachers and students to respond to these differences and thus close the learning gap or offer different learning experiences for those who are learning at an accelerated rate. When the impact is less than desirable, we have to respond by adjusting our instruction. Louder, longer, and more of the same is not an appropriate approach. Through careful analysis of and reflection on the data generated from formative evaluations, teachers must examine what worked and what didn't work, talk with colleagues, and redesign the learning opportunities for students. The engagement of this type of professional dialogue can be done during grade-level and content-level team meetings. For example, grade-level teams provide opportunities for teachers to collaboratively identify what worked in their colleagues' classrooms, regardless of the content, and consider these ideas for use in their own classrooms. In content-level teams, teachers can take about specific approaches to specific topics within the discipline of science. An eighth-grade science team meeting can discuss the most effective approaches for teaching Coulomb's Law, for example.

As we have noted, there is no one right way to teach science, and there are a lot of things that science teachers do that are effective. Designing learning opportunities, monitoring for impact, and then making adjustments represent the hallmark of effective teachers. Let's look at a formal way to monitor impact: response to intervention (RTI).

> Effect size for response to intervention (RTI) = 1.29

The evidence for RTI is significant, making this approach one of the top influences studied thus far. And, yes, RTI is an appropriate approach for science, not limited to only mathematics and literacy.

RTI is a multi-tiered system of support that is grounded in quality core instruction and referred to as *Tier 1*. Learners who do not respond to this quality core instruction are further supported by small-group intervention, referred to as *Tier 2*. When even more intensive support is needed, learners are then provided with *Tier 3*, or individual interventions. There are several components of an effective RTI effort relevant to science instruction, which combine to produce the impact seen in studies. A comprehensive discussion of RTI is beyond the scope of this book but available through other resources (e.g., Fisher & Frey, 2010). With regard to visible science learning, it is important to note that evaluation of learning provides insight into what additional learning experiences students need to be successful in science learning. Our job as teachers is to make the adjustments necessary to create that success for every learner in our classrooms.

Quality Core Instruction

RTI efforts are based on the expectation that students receive quality core instruction in the science classroom as part of their ongoing participation in school. Also known as *good first teaching*, quality core instruction constitutes Tier 1 of RTI efforts. Tier 1 instruction in science includes the use of strategies that work best at the right time in the learning process (i.e., surface, deep, or transfer). Science teachers who implement high-quality instruction, based on the influences on achievement outlined in this book, and then monitor the impact of those actions will find that fewer and fewer students need the extensive support beyond Tier 1 offered through RTI. To our thinking, quality core science instruction includes at least the following:

- Teacher clarity on, and communication about, the learning intentions and success criteria in the science classroom

- Student ownership of the expectations for learning through the co-construction of success criteria

- The acquisition and consolidation of surface learning that results in a strong conceptual understanding of science content knowledge and process skills

- Small-group learning based on instructional needs rather than perceived ability; this includes the adjustment of the difficulty and complexity of tasks to find the right level of challenge for learners

- Spaced (rather than mass) independent practice with effective feedback

- Collaborative learning opportunities on a daily basis so that learners can extract relationships between concepts (i.e., deep learning)

- Problem-based teaching that supports learners' transfer of content knowledge and processes to new contexts, scenarios, or problems

Progress Monitoring

Progress monitoring provides the necessary information to the teacher and learner regarding student response to quality core instruction. Earlier in this chapter, we discussed pre-assessments, post-assessments, and making thinking visible so that we can determine our impact on student learning. In addition to simply determining impact, each of these assessments allows teachers to monitor the progress of their learners. To adapt a commonly used saying that relates evaluation to cooking, progress monitoring is when the cook tastes the soup. Final evaluation is when the guest tastes the soup. Teachers can ascertain whether or not the lessons they designed and delivered made a difference long before the students complete a final evaluation or post-assessment. And then, of course, teachers can take the necessary next steps. Pre-assessments in science are important for identifying students who are in need at the outset of the year, but progress monitoring tools ensure that students' needs are noticed throughout the year as well. The progress monitoring tools that teachers use can result in students' receiving supplemental or intensive interventions.

Supplemental and Intensive Interventions

RTI focuses efforts on providing evidence-based interventions for students who do not respond to quality core instruction (also known as Tier 1) in the science classroom. In the language of RTI, students can receive Tier 2 or Tier 3 interventions, or a combination of the two tiers. This multi-tiered system of support can result in improved student learning, not just in literacy and mathematics but in the science classroom as well. As discussed earlier in this chapter, providing the necessary Tier 2 and Tier 3 interventions requires that teachers notice when students do not respond (i.e., when the impact is insufficient) and then change the instruction or intervention to reach the desired science learning outcome. The two levels of response are

1. Tier 2, also known as *supplemental interventions*
2. Tier 3, also known as *intensive interventions*

In Sarah Lucero's fifth-grade class, four students have been identified through a pre-assessment as needing additional instruction or intervention in communicating data using appropriate graphical representations and metric measurements. This is a power standard in fifth-grade and is a significant foundational skill for later science learning, as well as mathematics learning. Put differently, Ms. Lucero must respond by making adjustments in her instruction to ensure that these students make the necessary gains in their learning. Ms. Lucero does not simply use drill-and-kill with these students, nor does she simply cut her losses and move on with other content. Instead, Ms. Lucero meets with these students on a daily basis to provide small-group, needs-based instruction that modifies the difficulty and complexity of tasks focused on communicating data using appropriate graphical representations and metric measurements. This small-group instruction occurs while the other learners in the classroom work collaboratively on a task that focuses on the same skill, but at a different level of independence. The rest of the class works collaboratively. When these four students are not with Ms. Lucero, they are working collaboratively with their peers, and other students are meeting with Ms. Lucero to focus on other learning needs highlighted by the pre-assessment.

This same approach is used in Marc Childers's high school physics class. Pre-assessment data suggested that five of his students in first period need additional support in solving inclined plane problems, due to a gap in both their conceptual understanding of net force and the mathematical skills necessary to engage in this type of problem solving. Rather than encouraging the students to drop the course or verbally criticizing the mathematics department, Mr. Childers develops tiered problems involving the development of a free-body diagram, the creation of net force equations, and the solutions for various scenarios (e.g., acceleration of the object, the coefficient of friction, the angle of inclination). However, like Ms. Lucero, Mr. Childers meets with the five students to provide supplemental intervention in the conceptual understanding of net force, as well as the mathematics necessary for solving problems involving inclined planes.

> Effect size for not labeling students = 0.61

Supplemental and intensive interventions have the potential to positively impact students' learning when they are based on accurate assessment data and when students have instruction that addresses their learning needs, not their label.

In general, Tier 2 interventions involve the teacher meeting with small groups of students while the rest of the class completes other tasks that support their progress toward the learning intentions and success criteria. These tasks should have the appropriate ratio of difficulty and complexity for their needs as well. Giving students busy work while a teacher meets with students who need additional support does not constitute RTI. Instead, students should be engaged in collaborative and productive science tasks that deepen their knowledge, while the teacher meets with small groups to address targeted needs in the science learning process. In some cases, small-group instruction does not allow for breakthrough results, and more intensive interventions are needed to fill the learning gap. Often, these interventions are provided by experts outside the classroom (e.g., special educators or English language learning specialists), but the science teacher must be involved in intensive interventions by providing clear learning intentions, success criteria, and evaluation of learning. The logistics of RTI can be complex, but the key message in this approach is that all students can learn if we are willing to examine our impact and adjust the learning environment accordingly.

Learning From What Doesn't Work

Video 5.3
The Role of Technology in the Teaching and Learning of Science

http://resources.corwin .com/vl-science

Thus far, we have focused our attention on influences that can positively impact students' learning in the science classroom. We have explored surface, deep, and transfer levels of learning and have noted that there are some things that work better at each level. We have also discussed the ways in which teachers can determine their impact on student learning, and then respond when the impact is not as expected. Now it's time to focus on some things that really don't work to build science content knowledge and process skills. We don't want teachers to undo all of their hard work by engaging in practices that are harmful or that waste valuable learning time. After all, instructional time is precious. Classroom teachers must know not only what works best but also what may be taking up too much of their instructional time without delivering an impact on student learning.

Good Strategy, Bad Timing

Through this book, we have addressed some touchy challenges in the teaching and learning of science. For example, we explicitly described the often contentious debate between direct instruction, inquiry-based teaching, and problem-solving teaching. Within the science education community, this debate can quickly polarize teachers. This is not helpful. What the research strongly suggests is that there is no one way to teach science, and there is no one way to learn science. Instead, it is all about timing. Teachers may use a perfectly good approach for teaching and learning science (e.g., inquiry-based teaching) but use it at the wrong time (i.e., during surface learning). Good strategy, bad timing. To be absolutely clear, we are not advocating for one particular approach over another. As we highlighted in Chapter 1, effective teachers do not hold any instructional strategy in higher esteem than their students' learning. Visible learning is a continual evaluation of one's impact on students. When the evidence suggests that learning has not occurred, the instruction needs to change (not the child!). This refers not to a specific strategy but to a location in the learning process.

Ability Grouping

Ability grouping in the science classroom does not yield results that would support the continued use of this specific practice. The effect size of ability grouping is 0.12, which is negligible in terms of impact, yet this tactic is common in many schools. In the elementary school classroom, learners are often ability grouped because of their reading and mathematics performance. As a result, they are, by default, ability grouped in science. In the middle and secondary classroom, learners find themselves in science classes based on their choice of mathematics classes. Yes, certain science disciplines (i.e., physics and chemistry) require a mathematical skill set for students to be successful. Why not embed that skill set in the learning of science?

Some people argue that ability grouping works for advanced students, even if it doesn't work for learners with a lower level of readiness. The problem is that this is not true. Ability grouping disrupts the learning community, socially ostracizes some learners, and compromises social skills, to name a few effects of this practice (Sapon-Shevin, 1994). And the effect on minority groups is much more serious, with more minority students likely to be in lower-ability classes destined to demonstrate low performance, often with the least effective teachers (Jimerson, 2001). Through our work with preservice teachers and practicing teachers, we have encountered many situations where teachers, whether in their practicum, student teaching, or own classrooms, have grouped students by perceived ability. On the surface, this appears to be efficient and therefore feels effective. Taking a grade level of students and giving one teacher the lowest-performing students, another teacher the average-performing students, and yet another the highest-performing students may be a popular strategy, but the evidence is clear that it is not the answer. The two most common forms of ability grouping are

- *Within-class grouping*, or putting students in groups based on the results of a single assessment
- *Between-class grouping*, or separating students into different classes, courses, or course sequences (curricular tracks) based on their previous academic achievement

> Effect size for small-group learning = 0.47

The risk in writing this is that some readers will overgeneralize. Within-class and between-class ability grouping should certainly be avoided. But *needs-based* instruction, with flexible groups, should not be eliminated.

Student-centered teaching, which bases instructional actions on students' understanding and then engages students in small-group learning, can be very effective. In fact, small-group learning has an effect size of 0.49—provided that the grouping is flexible, not fixed.

The key to this approach is the condition that the groups change, and the instruction must match the needs of the learner. Let's look at the difference as it occurs within the same school. In one sixth-grade science classroom, the teacher administered a pre-assessment on structural and behavioral adaptations and grouped her students based on their scores. The students with the lowest scores were in one group, students with slightly better scores formed a second group, and so on. The teacher then met with the groups over several weeks, providing instruction on structural and behavioral adaptations to each group. Sounds familiar and logical, right? It just didn't work. The post-assessments were no different from the original samples. The lowest-performing learners were still the lowest, but their scores inched up a barely perceptible amount. That was a lot of work for very little benefit.

Down the hall, another sixth-grade teacher administered the same pre-assessment. She then analyzed the patterns of error found in her students' responses and continually regrouped students daily based on their error patterning. On one day, she met with a group of students who needed guidance with conceptual understanding of adaptations and what role they play in the survival of animals, and then she met with another group of students who needed support with relating this learning to specific habitats beyond their own community. These learners did not have a perspective beyond their own backyard. On another day, she focused her small-group instruction on students who needed additional support in making inferences based on data from a variety of sources. In this second classroom, learners' post-assessment scores significantly improved within each group.

The important difference between these two classrooms is the way in which each teacher used her instructional time. Each teacher had the same amount of time, the same content in which students needed to engage, and the same data available to her at the onset of this unit of study. However, in the second classroom, the groups changed, and the instruction matched the specific needs of the learners.

Again, student-centered science teaching, which bases instructional actions on students' understanding of science content and their fluency in specific process skills and then engages students in small-group learning, can be very effective. Small-group instruction is effective, but not when the intervention for the students is the ability of the group. The groups have to be flexible, so that the instruction each group receives aligns with the students' performance and understanding.

Matching Learning Styles With Instruction

How many times have you been asked about your learning style? How often have you heard colleagues make reference to their learning style? This idea is prolific in our schools and classrooms, frequently perpetuated by teacher preparation programs and teacher resources around the globe. Granted, there may very well be differences in how we prefer to access and share information, and that preference may change in different situations with different groups of people, but teaching students based on our perception of their particular type of intelligence or style is of very limited value. In fact, the effect size is 0.17. Matching instruction with a perception of a learning style is not going to radically raise student learning in science. There is just little evidence that students can be classified into various learning styles (e.g., visual, kinesthetic, auditory) when they need to be skilled in many learning strategies and styles; teachers may need to use many strategies to ensure that all students are learning. This does not mean that we should ignore student interests or preferences, as this can jeopardize the student-teacher relationship ($ES = 0.52$). Instead, we should provide quality core instruction that implements what works best. Then we should acknowledge individual interests and preferences, allowing learners to demonstrate their learning through multi-model evaluations that make thinking visible. Let's not label students, especially with learning styles; again, avoiding labeling has an effect size of 0.61. We should instead focus on instructional routines and habits that will ensure that all students learn at high levels. Teachers may need to use multiple methods to capitalize on multiple ways of learning, but the mistake would be to rigidly categorize students into one or more learning styles.

Test Prep

Test prep, including teaching test-taking skills, is another area where there is insufficient evidence to warrant continued use. The effect size is 0.27, which translates to roughly half a year of achievement. We've all done it, of course, because there is an appeal to one's surface logic to teaching students generic test-taking skills. But test-taking preparation just wastes a lot of precious time. Instead, we should include learning and test-taking skills as an integral part of every lesson (not as a separate subject)—focusing on teaching students the content and how to learn this content—as this has been shown to be much more effective in increasing student achievement on external measures of success. That's not to say that students shouldn't understand the format of the test; however, that instruction takes only a short time. Students should also be taught how to best prioritize time spent doing any task, as this can be a critical test-prep skill—but, again, we should do this within the context of the regular lessons—not as some standalone skill. Test prep and teaching test-taking skills are consuming significant numbers of instructional minutes, despite the fact that we know that there is no evidence that these accountability measures are going to inherently improve instruction or learning (Hattie et al., 2016). Studying content, and how to learn this content, especially by using effective study skills techniques (with an effect size of 0.63), will pay much better dividends than trying to figure out how to beat the test.

Homework

The final lesson we offer with respect to learning from what doesn't work, despite the fact that there are other issues we could explore, focuses on homework. Overall, homework has little impact on students' learning, with an effect size of 0.29. In this case, it's worth it to examine the value of homework at different grade levels. At the elementary level, homework has a limited impact on student learning, with an effect size of 0.15, whereas at the high school level, the effect size is 0.64. The major reason for this difference comes from the nature of homework and who does it. Homework that provides another chance to practice something already taught and for which a student has the beginnings of mastery can be effective (and much high school homework is of this nature), but homework that involves new materials, projects, or work with which a student may struggle when alone is least effective (and too much elementary homework is of this nature). And if the parents do the homework, which is more common in elementary school, the parents are learning a lot more science, and their children are not.

Importantly, homework may not be the answer to students' achievement, and efforts to raise the rigor of schooling by assigning more independent learning that students complete at home are misguided and potentially harmful. Students can succeed just as much based on what they do in school. Do not ask them to create a school at home, where many students will need adult expertise; while nearly all parents want to help their students, some do not know how. Again, as it is worth repeating, homework may not be the answer to students' achievement, and efforts to raise the rigor of schooling by assigning more independent learning that students complete at home are misguided and potentially harmful.

Conclusion

This last part of this chapter has focused on actions that do not work. We could have also focused on the finger-pointing common in some schools, turning this into a laundry list of "yeah, but" statements. Yes, mobility has a negative impact on students' learning, as does summer vacation. Hattie (2012) noted that about 50% of the achievement variation found in schools is attributed to student characteristics and demographics. Unfortunately, in many schools, that 50% gets all the attention. In many cases, this 50% becomes the scapegoat for less than desirable outcomes. After the students themselves, teachers have the biggest impact on student achievement, followed by school effects, the principal, parents, and the home. This is really, really important: A significant amount of the variance in student achievement is attributed to teachers. What we do matters—a lot. The previous four and a half chapters zeroed in on how to get the maximum achievable results from the variance attributed to teachers. Put differently, what works best?

Video 5.4
Clarity About Our Impact

http://resources.corwin.com/vl-science

If you do the math, learners spend about one-third of their waking time in school. That means we have a fraction of our learners' time available to produce the greatest learning gains possible in the science classroom. That means we have to

1. Focus on what works best, not just what works, in teaching and learning science.

2. Develop challenging tasks that align with where students are in the learning process: surface, deep, or transfer.

3. Adjust those tasks so that learners are engaged in the right amount of rigor, or difficulty and complexity, to meet their needs.

4. Make thinking and learning visible to both the learner and the teacher, so that adjustments can be made in instruction that meet the learning needs of each student.

5. Know our impact.

What science teachers do matters!

Reflection Questions

1. How do you determine your impact on student learning? What data do you generate that could be used to determine your impact? What changes might you make after reading this chapter?

2. How do you make student thinking visible? What changes could you make to your evaluations that would make student thinking more visible to you and the learner?

3. What do you, your colleagues, or your school do to support learners who do not make the expected gains in their science learning? What supplemental and intensive interventions are available to your learners? What additional support might you offer to your learners?

4. What are the next steps for you? What will you do with the information in this book? What changes might you make to your science teaching?

References

Ausubel, D. P. (1968). *Educational psychology: A cognitive view*. New York, NY: Holt, Rinehart & Winston.

Bass, J. E., Contant, T. L., & Carin, A. A. (2009). *Teaching science as inquiry* (11th ed.). New York, NY: Pearson.

Bereiter, C. (2002). *Education and mind in the knowledge age*. Mahwah, NJ: Lawrence Erlbaum.

Biggs, J. B., & Collis, K. F. (1982). *Evaluating the quality of learning: The SOLO taxonomy (structure of observed learning outcome)*. New York, NY: Academic Press.

Bransford, J., Brown, A. L., & Cocking, R. R. (2000). *How people learn: Brain, mind, experience, and school* (Expanded ed.). Washington, DC: National Academies Press.

Brookhart, S. M. (2008). *How to give effective feedback to your students*. Alexandria, VA: ASCD.

Bruner, J. S., Goodnow, J. J., & Austin, G. A. (1986). *A study of thinking* (2nd ed.). New York, NY: Routledge.

Cazden, C. (2001). *Classroom discourse: The language of teaching and learning*. Portsmouth, NH: Heinemann.

Coll, R. K., & Lajium, D. (2011). Modeling and the future of science learning. In M. Khine & I. Saleh (Eds.), *Models and modeling: Cognitive tools for scientific enquiry* (pp. 3–21). Dordrecht, The Netherlands: Springer.

Crismond, D. P., & Adams, R. S. (2012). The informed design teaching and learning matrix. *Journal of Engineering Education, 101*(4), 738–797.

Dean, D., & Kuhn, D. (2007). Direct instruction vs. discovery: The long view. *Science Education, 91*(3), 384–397.

DeLashmutt, K. (2007). *A study of the role of mnemonics in learning mathematics* (Summative projects for MA degree). University of Nebraska–Lincoln. Retrieved from http://digitalcommons.unl.edu/mathmidsummative/19

Deming, D. J. (2017, June). The growing importance of social skills in the labor market. *NBER Working Paper No. 21473*. Cambridge, MA: National Bureau of Economic Research. Retrieved from http://www.nber.org/papers/w21473

Driver, R., Squires, A., Rushworth, P., & Wood-Robinson, V. (1994). *Making sense of secondary science: Research into children's ideas*. London, England: Routledge.

Duschl, R. A., & Osborne, J. (2002). Supporting and promoting argumentation discourse in science education. *Studies in Science Education, 38*, 39–72.

Estes, T. H., Mills, D. C., & Barron, R. F. (1969). Three methods of introducing students to a reading-learning task in two content subjects. In H. L. Herber & P. L. Sanders (Eds.), *Research in reading in the content areas: First year report* (pp. 40–47). Syracuse, NY: Syracuse University Press.

Fisher, D., Everlove, S., & Frey, N. (2009). Not just another literacy meeting. *Principal Leadership, 9*(9), 40–43.

Fisher, D., & Frey, N. (2010). *Enhancing RTI: How to ensure success with effective classroom instruction and intervention.* Alexandria, VA: ASCD.

Fletcher, J. D., & Tobias, S. (2005). The multimedia principle. In R. E. Mayer (Ed.), *The Cambridge handbook of multimedia learning* (pp. 117–134). New York, NY: Cambridge University Press.

Freedman, M. P. (2000). Using effective demonstrations for motivation. *Science and Children, 38*(1), 52–55.

Garcia, M. (2016). *Space debris and human spacecraft.* Retrieved from https://www .nasa.gov/mission_pages/station/news/orbital_debris.html

Gilbert, J. K. (2004). Models and modelling: Routes to more authentic science education. *International Journal of Science and Mathematics Education, 2*(2), 115–130.

Gilbert, J. K., Boulter, C. J., & Elmer, R. (2000). Positioning models in science education and in design and technology education. In J. K. Gilbert & C. Boulter (Eds.), *Developing models in science education* (pp. 3–17). Dordrecht, The Netherlands: Springer.

Goddard, R. D., Hoy, W. K., & Hoy, A. W. (2000). Collective teacher efficacy: Its meaning, measure, and impact on student achievement. *American Educational Research Journal, 37*, 479–507.

Griffin, M. M., & Robinson, D. H. (2005). Does spatial or visual information in maps facilitate text recall? Reconsidering the conjoint retention hypothesis. *Educational Technology Research and Development, 53*, 23–36.

Hastie, S. (2011). *Teaching students to set goals: Strategies, commitment, and monitoring* (Unpublished doctoral dissertation). University of Auckland, New Zealand.

Hattie, J. (2009). *Visible learning. A synthesis of over 800 meta-analyses relating to achievement.* New York, NY: Routledge.

Hattie, J. (2012). *Visible learning for teachers: Maximizing impact on learning.* New York, NY: Routledge.

Hattie, J. A. C., & Donoghue, G. (2016, August 10). Learning strategies: A synthesis and conceptual model. *Nature/NPJ: Science of Learning.* doi:10.1038/npjscilearn.2016.13

Hattie, J., Fisher, D., & Frey, N. (2017). *Visible learning for mathematics: What works best to optimize student learning.* Thousand Oaks, CA: Corwin Press.

Hattie, J., & Timperley, H. (2007). The power of feedback. *Review of Educational Research, 77*(1), 81–112.

Hattie, J. A. C., & Yates, C. R. G. (2014). *Visible learning and the science of how we learn.* New York, NY: Routledge.

Hester, K., & Cunningham, C. (2007, June). *Engineering is elementary: An engineering and technology curriculum for children.* Paper presented at the ASEE 2007 Annual Conference & Exposition, Honolulu, HI. Retrieved from https://peer .asee.org/1469

Horton, P. B., McConney, A. A., Gallo, M., Woods, A. L., Senn, G. J., & Hamelin, D. (1993). An investigation of the effectiveness of concept mapping as an instructional tool. *Science Education, 77*, 95–111.

Howard, L. (2010). *Five easy steps to a balanced science program for secondary grades.* Englewood, CO: Lead + Learn Press.

Hoy, W. K., Sweetland, S. R., & Smith, P. A. (2002). Toward an organizational model of achievement in high schools: The significance of collective efficacy. *Educational Administration Quarterly, 38*(1), 77–93.

Huang, T., & Franzus, B. (1984). The vitamin C debate. *National Forum, 64*(1), 19.

Jeon, K. (2012). Reflecting on PEMDAS. *Teaching Children Mathematics, 18*(6), 370–377.

Jerald, C. D. (2007). *Believing and achieving* (Issue brief). Washington, DC: Center for Comprehensive School Reform and Improvement.

Jimerson, S. R. (2001). Meta-analysis of grade retention research: Implications for practice in the 21st century. *School Psychology Review, 30*(3), 420–437.

Johnson, D. W., & Johnson, R. T. (1999). *Learning together and alone: Cooperative, competitive, and individualistic learning.* Boston, MA: Allyn & Bacon.

Kapur, M. (2008). Productive failure. *Cognition and Instruction, 26*(3), 379–424.

Kapur, M. (2014). *Failure can be productive for teaching children maths.* Retrieved from http://theconversation.com/failure-can-be-productive-for-teaching-children-maths-22418

Karp, K. S., Bush, S. B., & Dougherty, B. J. (2014). 13 rules that expire. *Teaching Children Mathematics, 21*(1), 18–25.

Klahr, D., Zimmerman, C., & Jirout, J. (2011). Educational interventions to advance children's scientific thinking. *Science, 333*, 971–975.

Lou, Y., Abrami, P. C., Spence, J. C., Poulsen, C., Chambers, B., & d'Apollonia, S. (1996). Within-class grouping: A meta-analysis. *Review of Educational Research, 66*(4), 423–458.

Manzo, A. V. (1969). ReQuest procedure. *Journal of Reading, 13*, 123–126.

Marzano, R. J. (1998). *A theory-based meta-analysis of research on instruction.* Aurora, CO: Mid-Continent Regional Education Lab.

Marzano, R. J. (2004). *Building background knowledge for academic achievement. Research on what works in schools.* Alexandria, VA: Association for Supervision and Curriculum Development.

Marzano, R. J., & Pickering, D. J. (2005). *Building academic vocabulary teacher's manual.* Alexandria, VA: Association for Supervision and Curriculum Development.

Marzano, R. J., Pickering, D. J., & Pollock, J. E. (2001). *Classroom instruction that works: Research-based strategies for increasing student achievement.* Alexandria, VA: Association for Supervision and Curriculum Development.

Mayer, R. E. (2003). The promise of multimedia learning: Using the same instructional design methods across different media. *Learning and Instruction, 13*(2), 125–139.

Mayer, R. E. (Ed.). (2005). *The Cambridge handbook of multimedia learning.* New York, NY: Cambridge University Press.

Mayer, R. E. (2011). *Applying the science of learning.* New York, NY: Pearson.

Medina, J. (2014). *Brain rules: 12 principles for surviving and thriving at work, home, and school.* Seattle, WA: Pear Press.

Michaels, S., O'Connor, M. C., Hall, M. W., & Resnick, L. B. (2010). *Accountable Talk® sourcebook: For classroom conversation that works* (v.3.1). Pittsburgh, PA: University of Pittsburgh Institute for Learning. Retrieved from http://ifl.lrdc.pitt.edu

National Research Council. (2007). *Taking science to school: Learning and teaching science in grades K–8.* Washington, DC: National Academies Press.

Nesbit, J. C., & Adesope, O. O. (2006). Learning with concept and knowledge maps: A meta-analysis. *Review of Educational Research, 76*(3), 413–448.

Newton, P., Driver, R., & Osborne, J. (1999). The place of argumentation in the pedagogy of school science. *International Journal of Science Education, 21*(5), 553–576.

NGSS Lead States. (2013). *Next generation science standards: For states, by states.* Washington, DC: National Academies Press.

Novak, J. D., & Gowin, D. B. (1984). *Learning how to learn.* New York, NY: Cambridge University Press.

Nuthall, G. (2007). *The hidden lives of learners.* Wellington, New Zealand: NZCER Press.

O'Donnell, A. M., Dansereau, D. F., & Hall, R. H. (2002). Knowledge maps as scaffolds for cognitive processing. *Educational Psychology Review, 14,* 71–86.

Palincsar, A. S. (2013). Reciprocal teaching. In J. Hattie & E. Anderman (Eds.), *International guide to student achievement* (pp. 369–371). New York, NY: Routledge.

Perkins, D. N., & Salomon, G. (1992). Transfer of learning. In T. Husén & T. N. Postlethwaite (Eds.), *The international encyclopedia of education* (2nd ed.). Oxford, England: Pergamon Press.

Protheroe, N. (2008, May). Teacher efficacy: What is it and does it matter? *Principal,* 42–45.

Ritchhart, R., Church, M., & Morrison, K. (2011). *Making thinking visible: How to promote engagement, understanding, and independence for all learners.* San Francisco, CA: Jossey-Bass.

Rosenshine, B., & Meister, C. (1994). Reciprocal teaching: A review of the research. *Review of Educational Research, 64,* 479–530.

Rutherford, F. J., & Ahlgren, A. (1990). *Science for all Americans.* New York, NY: Oxford University Press.

Sacks, O. (2001). *Uncle Tungsten: Memories of a chemical boyhood.* New York, NY: Knopf.

Sapon-Shevin, M. (1994). *Playing favorites: Gifted education and the disruption of community*. Albany: State University of New York Press.

Smith, I. (2007). *Sharing learning intentions*. London, England: Learning Unlimited.

Sweller, J. (2005). Implications of cognitive load theory for multimedia learning. In R. E. Mayer (Ed.), *Cambridge handbook of multimedia learning* (pp. 19–30). New York, NY: Cambridge University Press.

Treagust, D. F., & Tsui, C.-Y. (2014). General instructional methods and strategies. In N. G. Lederman & S. K. Abell (Eds.), *Handbook of research on science education: Volume II* (pp. 303–320). New York, NY: Routledge.

Virginia Department of Education (VDOE). (2012). *Practices for science investigation: Kindergarten-physics progression*. Richmond, VA: Author.

Wandersee, J., Mintzes, J., & Novak, J. (1994). Research on alternative conceptions in science. In D. Gabel (Ed.), *Handbook of research on science teaching and learning* (pp. 177–210). New York, NY: Macmillan.

Wilfong, L. G. (2012). The science text for all: Using textmasters to help all students access written science content. *Science Scope, 35*(5), 56–63.

Zembal-Saul, C., McNeill, K. L., & Hershberger, K. (2012). *What's your evidence? Engaging K–5 children in constructing explanations in science*. Boston, MA: Pearson.

Zepeda, C. D., Richey, J. E., Ronevich, P., & Nokes-Malach, T. J. (2015). Direct instruction of metacognition benefits adolescent science learning, transfer, and motivation: An *in vivo* study. *Journal of Educational Psychology, 107*(4), 954–970.

Index

A SAGE Publishing Company

Helping educators make the greatest impact

CORWIN HAS ONE MISSION: to enhance education through intentional professional learning.

We build long-term relationships with our authors, educators, clients, and associations who partner with us to develop and continuously improve the best evidence-based practices that establish and support lifelong learning.

Solutions you want. Experts you trust.
Results you need.